Asbury Park: *A West Side Story*

A Pictorial Journey Through the Eyes of
Joseph A. Carter, Sr.
Photographer 1917-1980

D0989097

Asbury Park, New Jersey

Asbury Park: A West Side Story
A Pictorial Journey Through the Eyes of Joseph A. Carter, Sr.
All Rights Reserved
Copyright © 2007 Madonna Carter Jackson

Outskirts Press
http://www.outskirtspress.com

ISBN-10: 1-59800-963-X
ISBN-13: 978-1-159800-963-7

Library of Congress Control Number: 2006934657

Outskirts Press and the "OP" logo are trademarks belonging to
Outskirts Press, Inc.

Printed in the United States of America

Asbury Park: *A West Side Story*

A Pictorial Journey Through the Eyes of Joseph A. Carter, Sr.
Photographer, 1917-1980

Asbury Park, New Jersey -1940's-1980's

Madonna Carter Jackson

Outskirts Press, Inc.
Denver, Colorado

Asbury Park: *A West Side Story*

Dedicated to my Mother,
Lenora Niblack Carter (1917-present)
"Daddy's favorite model, business manager, and supporter"

The Duchess

INTRODUCTION

*I*t has been twenty-six years since my Father, Joseph A. Carter, Sr., passed away on April 3, 1980. There hasn't been a day gone by that I haven't thought about, heard or saw something that reminded me of him.

The photographs in this book were taken in Asbury Park, New Jersey during the time period of the early 1940's through 1980. Six weeks before he passed away of cancer of the pancreas, photography had been his passion in life. Capturing the memories of individual's family celebrations, birthdays, weddings, funerals, presentations of awards, openings of new businesses, clubs and organizations' special events, community church auxiliaries' social and fraternal events, and portraits were his specialties.

This book of pictures is not meant to be a historical fact book; I see it as a small portion of a collection of photographs of people, places, and events that validate the African American celebrated life in Asbury Park, New Jersey sixty-seven years ago. For twenty-six years, I have cared for this collection consisting of hundreds of 4x5, black and white negatives. These images may have been destroyed or lost forever had I not taken a personal interest in them. They have survived through the winters and summers of rain, heat, and hurricane threats while I lived in sunny Florida. Some of the negatives had started to fade and spot from age, and because I only have negatives, most of the pictures in this book will not have the finished and retouched quality that my father provided to his customers, but I thought the subject at this point was more important.

Asbury Park today is not the Asbury Park of yesterday, but this is not a book to discuss the climate of existence in the one square mile town that I grew up in. If by viewing these pictures, you have some revelation of what could be, or better yet, what it should be, go for it! There are several books that tell the history of Asbury Park and its founding forefathers. In Asbury Park: A West Side Story, you will see me and my family in the early days of Asbury Park. The backgrounds of most of the pictures tell you where and about when the photos were taken. Landmarks that were once icons of the City, are

now gone and are today's ruins, or have been completely replaced.

You will see Springwood Avenue on the West Side, the beach front, the Boardwalk, and Ocean Grove on the Southeast. There are photographs of businesses that were either owned or operated by African Americans, or simply where African Americans frequented.

The reason I saved these negatives from the silver extraction system, is that I knew one day, the photography by Joseph Carter would be needed to document the positive existence of a media neglected people.

There are photos in this book that were taken when I was just a baby, and others that were taken when I was a little girl of two through thirty-two years of age. Each photo that is in this book has a memory attached that reminds me of my family and life in Asbury Park. This is my **West Side Story** through the lens of my father's camera.

Joseph A. Carter, Sr., Photographer

1960s

Carter's Studio located at 1207 Springwood Avenue Asbury Park, New Jersey.

Asbury Park, New Jersey is a one square mile city on the Jersey Coast of the Atlantic Ocean. With a beautiful ocean to its east, New York City to its North, the search for a better life is seen through the lens of my father's camera. My parents, Joseph A. Carter and Lenora Niblack Carter migrated from Florida to the Northeast in the early 1940's to begin their lives of things hoped for. As a photographer, he took photographs of the people and places in Asbury Park chronicling an era of African American History. I have taken these images of my parents past and remembered my childhood, and now I want to share these memories and precious moments. I have included blank lines for you to jot down whatever you remember about these times, or simply use them to start collecting your own memories about your hometown.

Birthday Party- 1950

Hines Birthday Party - 1950

I'm the little girl in the white dress sitting front row and in the middle of everyone.
I was about two years old, and I remember that moment.
I was told that only one other child is still alive.

The first " Carter's Photo Studio" in the late 1940s was next door to the State Pool Parlor on Springwood Avenue, Asbury Park, New Jersey.

*I*n 1950, I was two years old, but I remember peeping through the drapes that my father used as a background for photographing portraits, and through the picture window of our home that doubled as a photographic studio. I remember seeing women dressed in white uniforms, and white shoes. Some of the men were dressed in white pants, and matching shoes, while others were dressed in black and white suits with shiny black patent leather shoes. They waited on the corner for the bus to take them across town to the hotels, and bed and breakfast rooming houses where they worked during the summer. I remember that on Friday night, they would go dressed in white, but would return dressed in silk and satin dresses. The ladies hair were silky shiny from a fresh hot press and curl. Some of the ladies would walk in and ask my dad to take a picture of them in their new outfits.

An 8x10, 2-5x7's and 6 wallets for $8.50. Black and White or Sepia Tone. It was exciting to see all these beautiful people all dressed up and wanting to have their picture taken. Fussing with their hair and makeup, I watched my father pose them in the most flattering positions. Making sure that their features and colors were captured with the perfect lighting and highlights.

1940's

*B*lack people in Asbury Park, worked hard, played hard, and always looked good. The most beautiful dresses you've ever seen. Satins and silks, some form fitted at the perfect length. Stiletto heels with French silk stockings, some with black lines running up the back of the legs. They look just like they stepped out of Vogue Magazine, or should have, because you and I know, in the 50's, there were no black people in the magazines.

After his children were asleep, Carter, as he was called, would go across the street with his camera and camera bag to take pictures of the night club goers. He would take a picture of a handsome couple, rush back across the street to his studio/apartment, and develop and print a slick black and white photo of the couple. He would have the picture back within an hour. He took hundreds of photos like that. He never put names on the negatives, but batched them by the name of the Club where he had taken the picture. Write me if you recognize anyone.

11

An unidentified man poses in front of the first "Carter's Photo Studio" in the late 1940's

I hope to add more names in a second publishing.

East of the Studio in the 50's was the *West Side Dining Room.* I remember the double door entrance with square window panes. Neat square tables with heavy starched table cloths. I don't remember ever eating there, but maybe you do.

Cuba's Night Club was the entertainment spot in the 50's and for several years before my parents moved to New Jersey. Names like Billy Eckstein, Cab Calloway, Billy Holiday, and local entertainers turned Springwood Avenue into the place to be on Friday and Saturday nights.

Visitors had their favorite local blues and jazz musicians that they would enjoy at Cuba's. Do you remember *Cuba's*?

I can remember hearing music loud at one point, then it seemed to fade away. I know now that it was the door opening and closing at the club. My memory is vague, but the sensation of the moment lingers with me. I listen to music today while I sleep.

1940's in
Asbury Park, New Jersey?

Right: Willie Niblack standing in front of Cuba's Night Club 1940's.

Below: Unidentified entertainer at Cuba's Night Club in the early 1940's.

When I was asked to write and submit a photograph for a monthly article that I write for the Shore African Magazine, and cover the theme: *"Women on the Move"* , look what I found! A woman most young people today have never heard of — Ms. Billy Holiday: (1915-1959). My father took this photo in the 40's at *Cuba's Night Club* located on Springwood Avenue in Asbury Park, NJ. I knew immediately who she was by the gardenias in her hair. They called her *Lady Day*, and her music was smooth, and sexy. Her lyrics were mostly motivated by her life's experiences. Songs like "Strange Fruit," was actually about a black man who she witnessed hanging from the limb of a Poplar tree by racists in the South.

In the photograph, a big jazz band of the early days was warming up while they waited to back her up when she performed her songs. Encourage your children to read her biography. Though her life and death was unfortunate and tragic, she was an African American woman who wrote most of her music. Her life will be remembered for ages, and this picture places her in Asbury Park on the West Side.

*W*rite your memories here..

People came from every corner of the shore area. Beach visitors from New York and Philadelphia, people from all nationalities crossed the tracks to the West Side, sometimes called "the dark side" of town. It was one of the favorite nite spots to listen to good jazz and blues, or simply be seen.

Miss Billy Holiday at Cuba's Night Club, Asbury Park, NJ in the late 1940s
(This negative was damaged by aging spots)

Singing, dancing, entertaining, or being entertained was a pleasure after a long week of working at the shore restaurants, and hotels. Making sure the rest of the world had conveniences during their stay at the the beach resort was a sun up to sun down job. Hospitality work was the only type of employment that most black people could get in the early days. If you had an education, you were either a teacher, principal in an all black school, a preacher, or you may have owned a beauty parlor, barber shop, soul food restaurant, candy store, or taught piano lessons to the neighbor-hood children. The world wars, times of depression, and the civil rights movements were widely documented periods of history in these times, but for Blacks in American, only the negative images of our lives would be seen in the newspaper, magazines, and on television.

Our choices were now greater. The opportunity to be more than we had ever dreamed was becoming a reality. At last we were now beginning to see the doors to a "promised land" open for us. But the doors were not opened all the way.

Write your memories here..

A Jazz and Blues band of the 1950's. On trumpet, Edward Watt, Sr.; on piano, Sam Pugh, and Andrew Brown on drums. Do you remember the other entertainers?

*W*rite your memories here..

*W*rite your memories here..

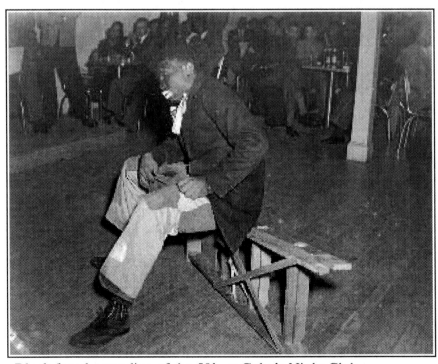

Black faced comedian of the 50's at Cuba's Night Club.

1950's Waitresses at Carver Hotel, Neptune, NJ

*W*rite your memories here..

1950's *W*aitresses & Head Waiter at Berkley Carteret Hotel,
Asbury Park, NJ

*W*rite your memories here...

*W*rite your memories here..

Photo taken in the late 1940's or 50's -Kitchen help at one of Asbury Park's Bed & Breakfast or Seashore hotel.

*W*rite your memories here..

Photo taken in the late 1940's or 50's -Kitchen help at one of Asbury Park's Bed & Breakfast or Seashore hotel.

1950's   Live entertainment at Cuba's Night Club, Asbury Park, NJ

*W*rite your memories here..

1950's   In front of Fisch's Department Store: a taxi driver waits for a customer on Springwood Avenue, Asbury Park, NJ

Soldiers pose in front of a MD's car on Springwood Avenue, Asbury Park, NJ

1940's - My mother was a seamstress and loved sewing. She would look in Steinbach Department Store windows and come home to create the same garment at a fraction of the cost.

*W*rite your memories here..

1940's -Doris Niblack-Wynn at the Carver Hotel in Neptune, NJ. She worked with Joe Carter as a camera assistant while Lenora, her sister, was giving birth to one of their children. When their daughter Madonna was born, Lenora stopped assisting with the *Bar Photography* and took transparent oil painting classes from Letty Thoms, a prominent artist from Long Branch, New Jersey. Within a short period of time, Lenora was able to do transparent oil painting of portraits taken in black and white.

*W*rite your memories here..

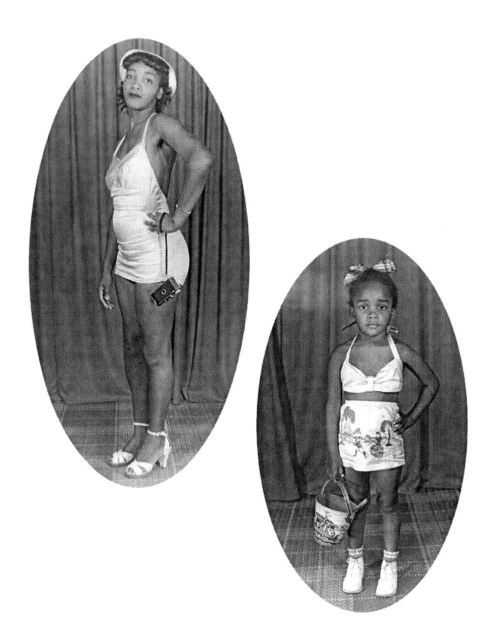

Unidentified customers taking photo in their bathing suit: Late 1940's

*W*rite your memories here..

1952 - This is just one of the many pictures that my father took of me and my brothers while we were growing up. I remember this moment because the photo was in our family album, and every New Year's Eve, we would look at old pictures. The story of how a customer came in for a portrait sitting on a Saturday morning, and in the middle of our Saturday morning cartoons on TV. We're sitting patiently while my father took the pictures of a woman who couldn't decide which side of her face was most photogenic. The cartoons were on, but the volume was down. We couldn't wait for the person to leave. After the customer left, my dad turned the sound back up, and took the picture of us enjoying our favorite Saturday morning programs. The television programs were most likely Howdy Doody, or Mighty Mouse, Sky King, Micky Mouse, or the Lone Ranger.

*Photo taken in the late1950's - Sunday morning on
Springwood Avenue. Chet's Restaurant in the background.*

*W*rite your memories here..

Photo taken in the late 1940's -Sunday morning on Springwood Avenue. A patron unable to make it home takes a nap on the Cuba's Night Club counter. The smell of stale smoke and empty beer bottles in the trash was a smell that lingered in the morning air.

*W*rite your memories here..

1950's Going to Church

The VanHuff's walk to Church on Sunday Morning
Springwood Avenue
Asbury Park, New Jersey

Photo taken in the late 1940's -The West Side Dining Room was located on Springwood Avenue, and was owned and operated by Mr. & Mrs. Robert Moore. Situated across the street from the Cuba's Night Club, it was a respected eating establishment by the community and tourist. I remember tables with crisp white linen table cloths and napkins. The sparkling clean windows never had a finger print on them, and the shinny crystal sugar bowls with matching salt and pepper shakers glisten in the sun light.

The Paramount Restaurant was owned and operated by an African American woman named Ethel Knight. It was located near the West Side Diner.

Write your memories here..

Late 1940's -Bobby Hill's Shoe Shine Parlor was located next to Jack's Shoe Repair. I can still hear the sound of the grinding wheel, and the smell of leather and shoe polish.

*W*rite your memories here..

There are dozens of photos that I don't have names or dates for, but I'm able to date them by the cars, or the clothes that people are wearing. Remember, I was only a child when most of these photographs were taken. I have very vague memories, all are of good people that I would consider historical icons from the Jersey Shore. I stimulated my thoughts, by sitting down and writing the names of all the people that were in my circle of life as a child. My memories are long, and take me as far back as 1951. It's amazing how long my list is. Try it, we will, with no doubt have some of the same names, but lets see. I'm really glad that I have finished this project when I did, who knows how long I'd be able to remember all that I have. One thing for certain, the pictures will always stir a memory when I forget. Start remembering your past. Good, bad, happy or sad memories should be documented for the future. Every contribution we have made to society is important for us to remember, not just as African American, but as being a part of the human race.

My memories about people and places in Asbury Park: 1948-1980

Springwood Avenue memories as a baby. My grandmother lived above *Kessler's* Grocers that was just across the street from *Fisch's Department Store.*

Fresh Meat Markets on Springwood Avenue with saw dust on floors.

Mr. Berger's Shoe Repair

Hosiery Department at Fisch's

Buster Brown Shoes at Fisch's

Bobby Hill Shoe Shine Parlor

Minnie and Mr. Cuba:

Elks Parades and the Giant Soldier

Walter Reade Theaters-
The Paramount,
Mayfair, Savoy, and Lyric Theaters

*W*rite your memories here..

Post Office: Corner of Main and Bangs-purchased saving stamps as a child

J J Newberry's Soda Fountain

Fischer Baking Company on Bangs Avenue: Best Hard Rolls in the World

Bed & Breakfast Guest during the Summers in Asbury Park: I don't remember the name of the hotel, but I do remember picking my grandmother up from work in the late afternoon. Loved running down the ally to the kitchen where she worked, and looking at all the people sitting on the porch enjoying the summer breeze from the ocean.

Bangs Avenue School

West Side Community Center

Asbury Park Boys Club

Bangs Avenue Play Ground Programs

Teachers I remember from Kindergarten to High School in Asbury Park:

K- Ms Beatle
1- Ms.Kemp
2- Ms. Carter
3- Mrs. Klinkenstein
4- Mr. Demby
5- Mrs. Moon
6- Ms. Burell

Ms. Lindeman- Home Economics
Mrs. Mount- Physical Education
7- Mr. Addeo, Mrs. Wilson, Mrs. Hagerman

How could I forget, my High School English teacher and writer- Mr. Thomas D. Williams, Author of the lovely novel "Cohesion" -1982.

*W*rite your memories here..

**Mentors and
Cherished Icons that I remember:**

Mr. Hyland Moore
Mr. Issac Young,
     Principals at Bangs Avenue School

Ms. Lola, Elks marching instructor

Marion Booker: my next door neighbor
who did my hair once a month.

Jennie Conti: Conti's Market Bangs
Avenue: taught me to cook Italian Style
for my 16th birthday.

Yvonne Eswick, piano teacher

Mrs. Bell, piano teacher

Mr. Freer, Janitor at Bangs Avenue
School

Crawley & Williams: delivered heating oil
rain or snow

Omega Psi Phi Fraternity Members that
supported Carter's Studio:

Ermon Jones, Floyd Scott, Jr.

Hunts Funeral Home
Leon Harris Funeral Home
Bunce and Carter Drug Store
Dorothy Toland Dance Studio
William Knuckles Electricians
Manhattan Dry Cleaners

*W*rite your memories here..

How many people in your neighborhood can you remember?

Mr. & Mrs. Holimon, the Deans, the Lewis family, Mr. John & Marion Booker, the Addeo's, the Smiths, Lawrence & Willie and their daughters Fern and Jackie Robinson, the Budds, Clarrits, Dr. Lorenzo Harris and Family, the Burrells, the Marshalls, Johnsons, Budds, Hunts, Vaccarros, Baileys, Butlers, Hayes family, and the three unrelated Carter families.

(All lived on Bangs, Ridge, and Summerfield Avenue

On the blank lines in this book, use them to write in your memories about Asbury Park, or memories about your home town. Twenty years from now, the significance of your time will be documented. With the new digital photography technology, it is easy for anyone to capture the moments of time. I'm proud of the photography that my father captured during his life.

A profound, and soul-stirring line from the novel, movie, and award winning Broadway musical, The Color Purple, by Pulitzer Prize winning author, Alice Walker speaks the heart of many.

"I'm poor, black, I may even be ugly, but thank God, I'm here!"

We were here in Asbury Park, NJ!

*W*rite your memories here..

1950s   Typical store fronts on Springwood Avenue, Asbury Park, NJ

1950s   Carver Hotel, Neptune, NJ

*W*rite your memories here..

The Carver Hotel 1950's

The Staff & Guest

Carver Hotel Bar Staff and Entertainers- 1950's

Carver Hotel Guest - 1950's

Beautician Banquet - 1950's

*W*rite your memories here..

1950's *R*einheart Inn, Asbury Park, NJ
(formerly the well known Waverly Hotel)

*W*rite your memories here..

1940's *B*elmont Hotel, Asbury Park, NJ

*W*rite your memories here..

*W*rite your memories here..

*1940's B*elmont Hotel,
Asbury Park, NJ

African Exotic Dancers
performed in the 1940's at the
Belmont Hotel and other night
spots.

1950's *F*ashion Show at the Belmont Hotel, Asbury Park, NJ

*W*rite your memories here..

1950's - The Almyra Tea Room - Named after the daughter of , David, Sr., and his wife Ester Parrott. Their son, Reverend David Parreott, Jr., shared his memories. The Tea Room was located at 1022 Mattison Avenue, Asbury Park, NJ. Inside, there was a dining room where breakfast, lunch and dinner was served. Mrs. Parreott was best known for her home made dinner rolls and fruit filled buns. It was a family affair from the making of the famous rolls to their delivery. Young David Parreott remembers having fun delivering the rolls, says he remembers hunger being stimulated by the delicious smell of the rolls. Copies of his parent's business licenses dating back to 1948. It was a family affair from the making of the famous rolls to their delivery. Young David Parreott remembers having fun delivering the rolls, says he remembers hunger being stimulated by the delicious smell of the rolls, so most dozens equaled eleven rolls.

Dr. Richard B. Carter, Sr., Pharmacist
Bunce & Carter's Pharmacy

I know there is a photograph of the Bunch and Carter's Drug Store in my father's collection, but for the life of me, I can't find it. I remember paper boxes that were hand packed with sweet vanilla ice cream. It was a treat to go into the store on Springwood Avenue when I was very young. Can you remember hearing the door bells ring as you came in? Dr. Richard Carter and his sister Ms. Alice Bunce ran the community pharmacy for years until the 1970 riots hurt them so badly that they would not continue.

They were the pharmacists that filled prescriptions for so many of us in the early days. When I was sick with one thing or the other, my mother said I would say, lets go to the Bunch of Carter's to get some medicine. I remember one specific time, I had a sore throat, my parents took me to the doctors who gave them a prescription for me. Dr. Carter seeing that I was not feeling well, told me to climb up on a stool at the counter, then he went behind the counter and made me a dish of vanilla ice cream. It was a miracle, I felt better almost immediately. When ever I eat vanilla ice cream now, I think of the family druggist at Bunce & Carter's on Springwood Avenue. I know you have memories to share about them! Few people knew how much they gave to the poor of the West Side community.

Manhattan Cleaners was next door the the Bunce & Carter Pharmacy and Ice Cream Parlor on Springwood Avenue.

The Manhattan 1 Hour Dry Cleaners was owned and operated by Charles Fauntleroy from 1946-1949. Mr. Joseph C. Davis became sole proprietor in 1949 and remained in business for until 1999. After the 1970 Riots, the dry cleaners was relocated to a Rail Road Avenue location, now named Memorial Drive.

In the 1950's many business people like the Fauntleroy's, and the Knuckle's actually lived on the second floor of their businesses. My grandmother lived upstairs over the Kessler's Food Market, and Berger's Shoe Repair Shop that was just across the street from Fisch's Department Store. There were alleys between the building that led to the back porches of these dwellings

Store clerk, Thomas Grant at Manhattan 1 Hour Cleaners

Remembering
Manhattan 1 Hour Cleaners
Springwood Avenue
Asbury Park, NJ.

Owner(s):
Mr. Charles Fauntleroy
1946-1949
and
Joseph C. Davis
(1949-1999)

Spotter & Presser, John W. Davis who is
the brother of the owner, Joseph C. Davis.

1950's   Springwood Avenue businesses: Rice Jewelers and Knuckle's Electric.
Families dwelled in the apartments upstairs.
The Bunce & Carter's Drug Store was two doors West of Knuckle's Electric.

*W*rite your memories here..

1950's Behind the storefront businesses on Springwood Avenue was another world. On any Saturday, the railings would be covered with sheets and laundry belonging to the families living on the second and third levels. There were large alley cats that would walk the railing without missing a step. Ringer style washing machines hummed as the water swished back in forth in the deep round wash tubs, and the smell of cleaning chemicals and bleach were always present. My grandmother would wash her porch every morning to keep the dust from coming in the back screened door. What a wonderful memory of my Grandmother, Mamie Clark-Niblack. I can hear her telling us kids to stay off the back railings. She would say, "somebody is gonna get killed falling off those old wooden railings."

West Side Drugs and Liquors located on the corner of Springwood Avenue and Atkins Avenue. Customer Angie Graham is greeted with a friendly smile from the pharmacist on duty. **1950s**

West Side Drugs and Liquors was located on the corner of Atkins and Springwood Avenue. My memories are of the friendly people that worked there. They sold just about everything. It was directly accross the street from the Turf Club, and east of the second Carter's Studio that was located at 1207 Springwood Avneue.

West Side Hardware Store was located at 1034 Springwood Avenue. The Berger's Shoe Repair and the Asbury Liquor Store was just next door. Maybe you have memories of these stores and their owners.

*W*rite your memories here..

One hour photography was done in the 1950s. Here the stylish
Mr. Robert Cooper, owner and operator of the Eureka Barber
Shop on Springwood Avenue, and an unidentified woman pose
for a photo at the Carver Hotel. How many songs do you
remember that were played on the "Juke Box" in the 1950's?

Write your memories here..

Dresses of the 1950's were colorful and frilly. While going through the hundreds of black and white negative, I came across photos of people that I remembered from my childhood. The lady on the right is Mercedes Batiste, the mother of one of my classmates.

*W*rite your memories here..

1950s- The Public Welfare Building in Asbury Park was used for wedding receptions.
Captured memories of the guest of Brides and Grooms was one way that people had
any photographs of themselves. Photography was still expensive, and considered a
luxury; thus, speculating a potential sale of candid pictures at weddings rendered boxes
of unsold photos. This building was located between Sylvan and Union Avenues.

*W*rite your memories here..

1950s- Families of all races would come to the studio to have their photos taken. My father didn't understand Spanish, but always got a smile. On the envelopes holding their negatives, he would write: Spanish Family, or friend of Louis.

*W*rite your memories here..

1947- Ms. Erma Brown proudly shows off her new television in the family room of her boarding house located on Ridge Avenue, Asbury Park. My parents, Joseph and Lenora stayed with her a few months before renting a studio apartment on Springwood Avenue where they established the first Carter's Photo Studio. Summer hotel and restaurant workers stayed in the Brown's three story rooming house during the summers.

*W*rite your memories here..

1948 - Lake Avenue, Asbury Park - It's a little after four in the afternoon in the month of August. Enjoying a balmy ocean breeze, with Ocean Grove in the background, my mother poses with my brother Butch. The excitement of the amusement rides and the music of the Merry-Go-Round that was just across the street, distracted my brother who was trying to get a look at the motor boat ride as it passes by.

Summer fun at the beach.
Asbury Park, NJ
1950's

Joe Carter and his son, Joe, Jr. at one years old.

After a long day's work,
Lenora and Joe would go
to the beach and cool off.
Asbury Park, NJ.

Spring 1948

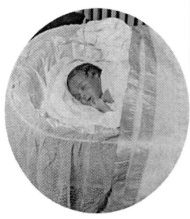

Then came Madonna
November 21, 1948
Now one of the baby boomers.

After moving to Bangs Avenue, my sister, Marshia Jefferson White attended school at Bordentown Manual Training School. I remember road trips to her school where we had picnics, and I would meet all her friends. By the time I was old enough to go to that school it had closed.

Just a note, the reason you don't see many pictures of my sister in this book is because she said she would sue me if I put her baby pictures in any type of book, so I am respecting her wish. But I know she is proud of this photo in her majorette outfit in 1954. *Below:* Summer Carter Family Portrait.

Boardentown Manual Training & Industrial School for Colored Youth 1886-1955. Ironically, a 1947 state legislation requiring integration caused the all black school to close. (L to R) Marshia Jefferson, Harriett, and Shirley.

During the late 40's, there was a family stationed at Fort Monmouth that my parents rented a spare bedroom to until they found their own home. The Mitchell's had one son at the time, but later they found their own home and added two more children to their family. They came and had a family protrait with the wife's mother who lived in Asbury Park.

The arrangement worked for both their family and mine, it helped with our finances, and helped a family stay together until they found their own home.

Just one of the sewing creations made by my mother.

She worked as a seamstress at the Walburn Sewing Factory on Cookman and Main Street making fine coats and children's' clothes.

During WWII, she made parachutes for the Air Force. Her career with the Amalgamated Garment Union and the US Garment Workers of America Union spanned over 20 years.

1521 Bangs Avenue ..wasn't like the houses on the hill - *referring to the new homes built in the 60's in Neptune, NJ.,*

but it was finally a home that didn't have damp and moldy rooms that caused her children to have phonomania every other week. My parents lived in that house from 1948-1980. The youngest son, Ernest Carter was born there. He is the one celebrity in the family, and a multi-talented musician. He took music and drum lessons from early child hood, and played at the Turf Club on Springwood Avenue before he was 16 years old.

Ernest started with his own group Tone, then played with another group Hot Ice with David Sancious. Later in his career, he played with Bruce Springsteen on one of his hit recording: **Born to Run**. Today he owns his own recording studio: Carter-Niblack Productions in San Leandro, California.

Joe Carter and portrait camera he put
together with used parts.
1950s

Carter's Photographic Studio
1521 Bangs Avenue
Asbury Park, New Jersey

Portraits, photo restoration, and
coloring was all done in our dining
room.

1960's - The Carter's at 1521 Bangs Avenue, Asbury Park, NJ 07712

1950s- Joe Carter working in home based business.
Carter's Studio developed by word of mouth. For every job he did for a new person, he would get another referral.

At one point at 1521 Bangs Avenue, my father wanted to purchase the house and have a studio, but one neighbor voted no for having a studio in the neighborhood. Even though there was a bar, grocery story and bakery in the neighborhood, Carter continued to take pictures from the house and locations within the community. For a long time, photography did not require a business license.

1950s- The Cities Service Station was on the corner of Ridge and Springwood Avenue. One of the stations's previous owners, Reverend Peek, used Carter's Studio for a family portrait after he did photographs of the grand opening of his gas station.

1950s- The Peek Family

1950s- Conti's Employees at the Horse Shoe Bar on Ridge Avenue, Asbury Park.

1950s- Employees of a meat market on Prospect and Bangs Avneue.

1950s- Church auxiliaries planned their annual booklets and banquet program that included photos of their members.

1950s- The Ministers Wives of Asbury Park, NJ.

1950s-The WCAP radio station, Asbury Park, NJ
Joe Carter was called to take pictures of presentation, and retirement events.

1950s- Mr. Robert Cooper owned and operated the Eureka's Barber Shop on Springwood Avenue, Asbury Park, NJ

He migrated from the south to become a successful entrepreneur and home owner.

1950's- Mr. Shelly operated the Shoe Shine Shop in the Eureka's Barber Shop on Springwood Avenue, Asbury Park, NJ

Eureka's Barber Shop did the hair processing for men, and stylish hair cuts for women..

1950's- Starting a business for yourself was an option for African Americans during the 1950's and 60's. Without a college education the wage potentials were limited. Innovative African Americans established small businesses. Needed and essential services proved to be profitable endeavors for most. Danny Harris of Neptune, NJ opened this Gulf Station.

*Do you remember paying **26** cents a gallon for gas?*

*W*rite your memories here..

Leon Harris and his son, Fortune Harris ran a Funeral Home that was located on Heck Street, Asbury Park, NJ. I remember going with my father to take pictures of people who were killed in an accident.

Mr. Harris and Mr. James Hunt of Hunt's Funeral Home both serviced the African American community during their time of need. My mother's family alone, used James Hunt's Funeral Home for her entire family: Mother, Father, two sisters, and seven brothers.

*W*rite your memories here..

_____

_____

_____

_____

_____

1950's - These are samples of occupations that African Americans put their hearts and souls into. Above: **Davis Sign Service** - The printing business has changed to the point these machines are obsolete. The sign makers in the 1950's knew the calendar of events in the community better and sooner than anyone. Below: **Jersey Coast, Inc. Produce Company** - An unidentified man proudly stands next to his new delivery truck.

1950's - Bea Toran owned and operated the Bea Toran's Hair Fashions on Springwood Avenue. She hosted several of the fashion and hair shows at the Elks Club, and Carver, and Berkly Carteret Hotel.

*W*rite your memories here..

The Conti's of Asbury Park: Salvatore, Louis, and Jenny Conti -
Conti's Market on Ridge and Bangs Avenue, Asbury Park, NJ. Jenny
taught me how to make real Italian Spaghetti Sauce.

Spanish people in Asbury Park loved having informal photographs taken to
send home to their families. I met children from many cultures as a child.
Some have become life long friends.

1950's -Students from the school system were taken on field trips to places like this bread factory. Fishers Bread Company. Do you remember these trips?

*W*rite your memories here..

*W*rite your memories here..

NOTE: This is one of my favorite with the whole family in 1953.

1950's - Even during Christmas, my father was called to take a picture of a family's memorable moment. Pictured here is a first Christmas as a family member for one of these little boys who was adopted. Gun and holster sets were popular for both boys and girls in the 1950's.

1950's - Snow storms in Asbury Park, NJ were called blizzards. Lenora Carter in the back yard at 1521 Bangs Avenue, Asbury Park, NJ

1950's - Joe Carter would take his children out after a heavy snow storm and take a picture for the year's Christmas card.

My parents had very little education, but they learned while their children learned, and they taught themselves how to make something out of little to nothing. I am thankful for all of my special memories through the photography of my dad. The camera was always a part of our everyday; while playing next door in John and Marion Booker's garage, or simply having breakfast during the week. Memories of my childhood and the people that lived in Asbury Park will forever be my fondest and most cherished treasures. Each photo stimulates the memory of the moment.

Late 1950s we always ate every meal together. I was the picky eater. I would sit for hours trying to eat three little green peas.

*T*his photograph was taken in front of the house that I grew up in at 1521 Bangs Avenue. My two brothers, Joe and Ernest Carter, and a neighborhood friend Louis Byrd were playing in the flood waters after a hard summer's rain. Our home was on the northeast corner of Bangs and Ridge Avenue that is located less than two miles west of the ocean, and one long block north of Springwood Avenue. I remember everyone saying that our street should have been named Springwood instead of Bangs.

The children have smiles on their faces as they frolic in the water, and they played for hours until the water finally receded. Although there was no real property damage, it reminds me that a storm like Hurricane Katrina that ravaged Louisiana and the Gulf Coast in 2005 could happen anywhere there is coastal property. I wondered if Asbury Park would be ready for a catastrophic disaster of that magnitude? Would all of its people — black, white, and yellow — be ready to meet the challenges of working together to survive?

The design of my home town had distinct dividing lines between the races. *I believe* that cultural divisions in America will inevitably cause our doom unless we are able to help one another regardless of race or class. Each and every American has something to bring to the table when survival is threatened. In every neighborhood, whether we know each other intimately, or just speak casually in passing, we should be able to band together in crisis, and think EQUAL and FAIR.

Do you remember the flood?

1960's - A tornado struck Bangs Avenue a few weeks before Easter in the 1960's ripping a two story house from its foundation, and tearing the roof off of the apartments behind 1521 Bangs Avenue. The roof fell on top of my brother Ernest's bicycle just seconds after he jumped off his bike to run onto his back porch. He was terrified by the sound of the wind, and all of the flying debris. Still today, he shutters when hearing high winds. There were no fatalities, but the property damage was high.

The photo above of Ernest Carter was on the cover of the New York Daily News.

87

1950's - The Omega's used Carter's Photographic Studio to cover many of their presentations and accomplishment within the city of Asbury Park, and Neptune, NJ. Pictured here, Mayor Ray Kramer, and Architect, Floyd Scott, make a presentation to Funeral Director, Leon Harris. The picture was taken inside the St. Stephens Church.

*W*rite your memories here..

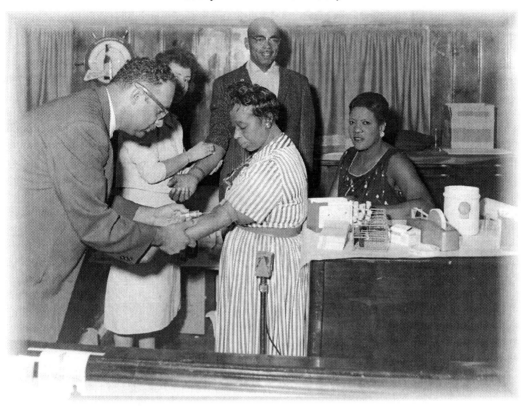

1950s - Dr. Lorenzo Harris takes blood from Mrs. Louise Hughes at a Blood Drive. Dr. Harris served as a community advocate, and City Councilman. Mrs. Hughes was a well know community activist who worked tirelessly for the children's welfare system.

*W*rite your memories here..

1954 Prom at Bangs Avenue School

Pictured at a Prom for Middle School students in the Bangs Avenue School Gym on Dewitt and Bangs Avenue are Sharon Harris, and Clifford Noland. Sharon is presently a teacher in the Asbury Park School System, and served as a Councilwoman in the City. She is the daughter of Dr. Lorenzo Harris who also served as a Councilman, and Mayor of Asbury Park. She will be remembered for her efforts to keep the historical Springwood Avenue's name the same. The city had changed it to Lake Avenue at one point after the 1970 riots.

Alumni of the Bangs Avenue School - Photo taken in the 1950s

1953 Kindergarden Class: Mr Moore was the principal.
This is Joe Carter, Jrs.' class photo taken by Joseph Carter, Sr.

The Hudson's
of
Neptune, NJ

Dance recitals at
Bangs Avenue School
1950s

Bangs Avenue School's stage was the center point of the school, dividing the North and South wings of the building. There is a book just waiting to be written about the historical white cement building on Bangs Avenue, Asbury Park, NJ.

Children in the community performed their talents on the Bangs Avenue School stage that was hosted by either the school, or an organization.

*W*rite your memories here..

Class picture taken at Bangs Avenue School. My uncle Donald Niblack is in this photo taken while he attended Bangs Avenue School. He was a baby when my grandparents migrated to NJ with their children in the early 1940's. He went on to Asbury Park High School and was an All State Basketball Player.

In the early 1950's Carter's Studio was used for group pictures at Bangs Avenue
School. Principal Issac Young was a great supporter. By word of mouth, the
services of Carter's Studio spread outside Asbury Park, Neptune, and neighboring cities.

Community women's groups and the PTA always documented their achievements
with photography. During the 50's, groups were formed for just about anything
that would help pool resources and generate ideas to expose the youth of Asbury
Park and Neptune to activities that would assist them in being successful citizens.

*W*rite your memories here..

1950s - Pictured here are teacher, parents, and women in the Asbury Park community who met, planned, and organized programs for the youth of Asbury Park.

*W*rite your memories here..

Picture here are Eugene Baity, teacher; Issac Young, Principal; and Dentist,
Dr. John Hayes at a meeting at Bangs Avenue School. (Late 1950's)

Educators, medical professionals, and community members signed proclamations, developed organizations, mentored students, and supported the efforts that ensured that African American children received equal education and training facilities.

*W*rite your memories here..

1950's - A group of teenagers and community leaders pose for a group photo at the West Side Community Center. The WCCC sponsored dozens of programs for young women, and men of color. They provided a charm class to teach etiquette and grace.

1960's - A group of teenagers and camp counselors pose for a group photo at the West Side Community Center. The WCCC sponsored dozens of programs for children. This is a group of children going to camp. One of the children in this picture grew up to become a NJ Federal Judge. Thomas Smith.

West Side Community Center Charm Classes were offered in the 1950's.

West Side Community Center Charm Class Certificate of Participation presented by Mrs. Robinson to Madonna Carter 1950's

1960's: West Side Community Center Head Start Class

Mr. Knuckles of Knuckles Electric Company was just one of the many philanthropists who financially supported the West Side Community Center's efforts to provide activities for the area's youth.

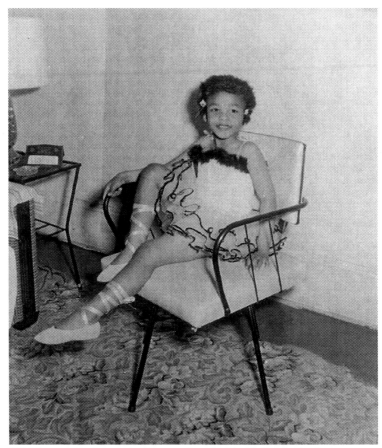

Waiting to perform at a Dance Recital is Stefanie Batiste.

Dance, the Arts, Sport, Personal Enrichment, and more was provided to the children of the West Side at the West Side Community Center

*W*rite your memories here..

1960's: Mayor Sharp James of Newark, NJ makes a contribution to the West Side
Community Center.

*W*rite your memories here..

Women's Clubs and Church Auxiliaries sponsored banquets and fund raisers at local hotels and restaurants. Dignitaries, athletes, entertainers, and prominent people were brought in to give motivational speeches to the community. Pictured here is Ms. Althea Gibson who was being welcomed at an organization's banquet. Ms. Gibson was a first in several areas of Tennis. She won 56 titles, and achived acclaims at the highest levels in the sport of tennis throughout her athletic career. In 1975, she became the NJ State Commissioner of Athletics and held that position for ten years. In 2003, she died at the age of 76 in East Orange New Jersey.

*W*rite your memories here..

Mr. George Butler, philanthropist, and community leader presents trees for a beautification project in Asbury Park.

*W*rite your memories here..

St. Peter Claver Catholic Church - Palm Sunday in the 1950's. Located on the corner of Springwood and Ridge Avenue. As a child, I loved looking at the beautiful paintings and art in their church. I visited with my neighborhood friend Penny Budd, whose brother was the Olympic Track Bronze Medalist, Frank Budd.

*W*rite your memories here..

Adam Clayton Powell, an African American Congressman for New York City from 1944-1970 is greeted by Reginald Pleasant of Asbury Park, who is a member of the Veterans of Foreign Wars located in Neptune, NJ. Danny Harris, businessman, and community activist is first on right next to Mr. Powell.

*W*rite your memories here..

Adam Clayton Powell listens tentatively as a member of the group discuss their business. The Veterans of Foreign War - 1950s

*W*rite your memories here..

The African American men and women belonged to groups that worked for the common cause of America. The Veterans of Foreign Wars used Carter's Photographic Studio to cover their prestigious events -Asbury Park 1950's

*W*rite your memories here..

Asbury Park was close to Ft. Monmouth and other US Government facilities that provided entertainment for soldiers stationed in New Jersey from all over the country. When asked to take pictures of performing bands, everyone was always ready to pose for a photo.

*W*rite your memories here..

African American Soldiers in the early 1950's

African American Soldiers in the early 1950's being entertained by local groups at the Post.

My father, Joseph Carter, captured Black History every day of his life through his photography. Selecting photographs from his archives was easy. This photo is from the negative of "The Thornton Sisters" of Long Branch, New Jersey.

I can still hear my parents praising the all girl jazz band of the 1950s. I knew that whenever I did publish: *Asbury Park — A West Side Story*, I would most definitely include the little girls band whose life's story is told in books written by the Thornton daughters Dr. Jeanette Thornton, and Dr. Rita Thornton.

Dr. Rita Thornton's book entitled, **A Suitcase Full of Dreams**: *"The Untold True Story of a Woman Who Dared to Dream."* It is a lovely narrative told from a mother's perspective about her daughter's lives. *A Suitcase Full of Dreams* is based on Yvonne Thornton's book: **The Ditch Digger's Daughters.** Because this book focused basically on their father, Dr. Jeanette Thornton and Dr. Rita Thornton pay tribute eloquently to their mother, Itasker Thornton, in their book.

"Do I raise my daughters to marry a teacher, a doctor or a lawyer, or do I raise my daughters to become the teacher, the doctor or the lawyer?" **Itasker Thornton**
Read more about the Thornton Sisters at these websites:

- http://www.doctorthornton.com/top.html
Is there a Doctor in the House: Dr. Yvonne Thornton
http://www.tnj.com/archives/2005/february2005/cover_story.php

Ray Charles in Asbury Park, NJ.
City policemen Charles Sandifer and my uncle George Niblack could have been brothers they looked so much alike, so some say the police officer is Charles, and others say it's George standing with area businessmen greeting and enjoying a moment with the musical idol. This picture was taken at the Convention Hall - Asbury Park, NJ (1960's)

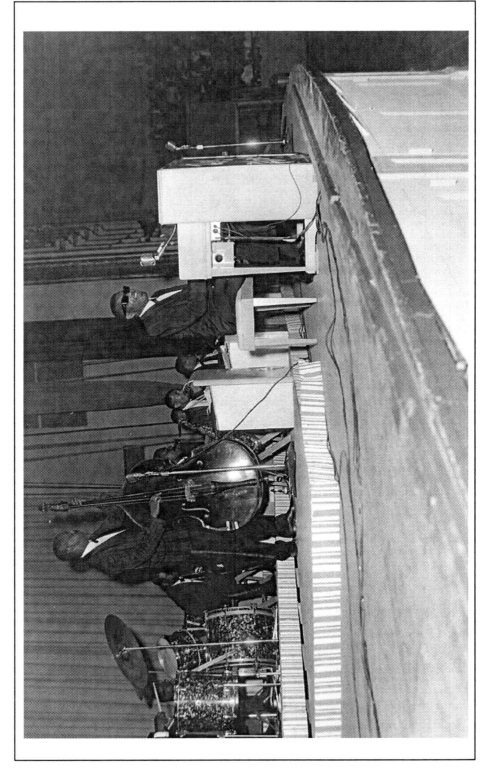

1960's - Asbury Park Convention Hall - Ray Charles Concert

Here is a 1950 photo of a concert band. I recognized our Asbury Drug & Liquor pharmacist, Cliff Johnson. I would love to know what the BB stood for.

The Rayletts
at the
Convention Hall
with
Ray Charles
1960

Police officer, Arthur
Harris and the Show
Promoter at the
Asbury Park
Convention Hall.

Ray Charles
Concert in
1960

Church Groups
Portraits
1950-60

Asbury Park is the home of many home grown musicians and singing groups. In the 1960s and 1970, several groups entertained for the Springwood Avenue Night Clubs. Below: Tony Maples and "The Squires".

*W*rite your memories here..

Gospel, Blues, Jazz, and
Rock & Roll : Asbury Park had
its own Home Town Musicians

1950-1960's

**Do you
remember any of these group?**

Sam Pugh's Band

1960's

**Do you
remember?**

Springwood Avenue early 1960's
Asbury Park, New Jersey

When you walked down Springwood Avenue, people filled the sidewalks. There were business signs as far as you could see, and as you walked from Atkins to Sylvan, you would smell deep fired chicken, shrimp, and french fries from one doorway, the well known smell of hair being straightened, or curled from the beauty parlors, and maybe stale beer as you passed the taverns. Ladies would walk real fast past the pool room because the young men hanging out would cat call the ladies as they passed by.

I remember always felling safe. I would walk to Fisch's Department store to purchase stocking s for my mother. Taupe, size 8-1/2, long. This was before panty hose.

As a teenager, Carl Williams, better know as Mr. Fashion, City Councilman, and former Mayor of Asbury Park greeted me gentlemanly as I passed through the men's ware department of the store. I remember the hosiery department being toward the back of the store, and they had boxes and boxes of neatly stacked stockings of all colors and sizes.

Springwood Avenue early 1960's
Asbury Park, New Jersey

Sunny Hunny Restaurant on Springwood Avenue

Shrimp Steaks
Shrimp Hamburgers
Shrimp Cakes

*W*rite your memories here..

Christmas at the West Side Community Center 1950's

The West Side Community Center is rich in history, and my memories don't even begin to tell the story of the WSCC. It is located on Dewitt Avenue in Asbury Park. Not only did the Center provide a place for young people to grow and develop into contributing citizens, it is where community leaders and residents from Asbury Park and Neptune gave their time and resources to the children. Children were exposed to all areas of development that would benefit them in their future.

When I was a child, they provided dancing and piano lessons. There were charm classes that showed young ladies how to walk, stand, and properly sit. Personal hygiene and health issues were demonstrated. There were children from every economic level working together, sharing tips of information that would be carried back to their homes, schools, and churches. In the 1950's and 60's, there were philanthropists who contributed funds to help finance events and special projects at the center.

*W*rite your memories here..

126

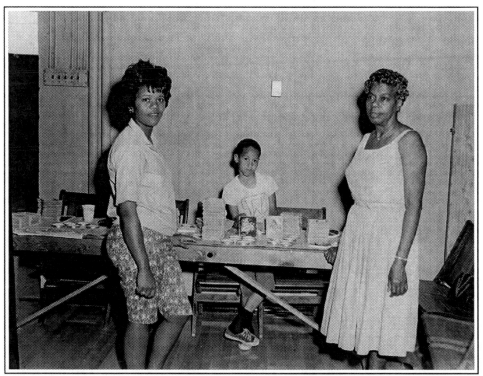

The Churches, Schools, West Side Community Center, Fraternal Organizations, and other Social Clubs provided various programs for Shore area
families. The "It takes a village to raise a child" theory was in effect long
before the titled book was written by Hilary Clinton. The ladies of Asbury
Park have generations of children, including myself, who are thankful for their
gifts of time and extended kindness.

I could write names for pages, but I will just roll call some to the names that
had major impact in my life. I know I will leave someone out, but that is where
my readers come in. Send me those names. When and if I ever reprint, I will
add those names to this dedication. But of all of the people that I remember I
must mention, Mrs. Gladys Johnson, school secretary, Ms. Kemp and Mrs.
Joan Carter, and Mrs. Mamie Moon who were Bangs Avenue School teachers
in the 50's. There was Ms. Lola, an Elks Lodge member who taught young
girls drill team wor I can barely remember their faces, but I remember their kind
and nurturing words that they had for all of us children growing up in Asbury
Park. They were all Pioneers in a time when we as a people were defining
ourselves a free and equal human beings. There is a song by Nicky Addeo, a
resident, singer and song writer from Asbury Park that says, "Through the Eyes
of Children, Healing and peace is realized."

These photographs were taken at the West Side Community Center and the ones on the opposite side were taken at a birthday party given for one of the Hine's Family Children. When I found this photo, I saw myself and my sister attending the party. This was about 1951. Look at the children of the 50's. Full of life, and ready to learn everything put in their paths. Though less than 50 years have passed, so many of these children are no longer here, but remembered as the wealth and hope of our society: The Children of the West Side of Asbury Park.

*W*rite your memories here..

*Hines Birthday
Party 1951*

Sisters: Marshia and Madonna

*T*om Thumb Weddings:

In the early 1960's, Tom Thumb weddings were organized by churches and community organization.

The contest was won by the child that sold the most advertising space in the organization's souvenir booklets.

*W*rite your memories here..

*T*om Thumb Weddings in the 1960's

*W*rite your memories here..

Mrs. Bell taught piano to young people from both Asbury Park, and Neptune, NJ. Her house is on Borden Avenue.

Mrs. Yvonne Eswick and music students. Left to right: Brenda Marshall, next two unknown students, Madonna Carter, remaining students's name unknown. *Maybe you remember them?*

In the next two pictures are of neighborhood children with my music teachers. Mrs. Bell, who lived on Mattison Avenue in Asbury Park; and Mrs. Yvonne Eswick, who lived on Bangs Avenue in Neptune. They taught the youth of Asbury Park and Neptune how to play piano. The gift given was the sharing of their talent and time with children all year long. These two ladies taught so much more than piano. They taught young girls and boys how to be ladies and gentlemen while going through their piano exercises.

I was probably their worst piano student, but my half hour with them was rewarding and memorable. Do you remember any of these children? The pictures were taken in the mid-50s. I recognize all of the faces, but their names escape me. Standing in the front row of Mrs. Bell's class is one of the Shore African American Magazine's Associate Editors, Lorraine Stone.

Bangs Avenue School in the early 1970's. May Day Celebration on the east play field that was used for grammar school programs.

Bangs Avenue School in the early 1970's. Gary Smith as May Day King is congratulated by School Board Member.

Bangs Avenue School May Day Celebration before the Middle School was built. The big field was used for out door event presented by the grammar school students. In the 50's and 60's, Bangs Avenue School made school more relevant and engaging for its children. At one point, I thought they were making a change to invent ways to make classes interesting, and were developing ways to make parents feel invited to be more involved, but some how things got off course. Children just don't want to go to school. They want to be entertained rather than entertain the world with their accomplishment. Teachers, Parents, and City Officials need to forget who is the reason for all the problems that we are having as a society, take a lead in coming together again to concentrate on making a group effort rather than a special interest effort.

Bangs Avenue School in the early 1970's. May Day Celebration Cultural Dancers

School Board Members attending a Bangs Avenue School May Day Celebration in the early 1970's. John H. Miller, was Vice President

Mrs. Louise Hughes is being sworn in by an Asbury Park City Official as Mayor Kramer looks on. She was the Director of the Child Welfare Department.

Mrs. Hughes, and Mr. James Hunt, of Hunt's Funeral Home are together at one of the local Churches for a community presentation of some sort.

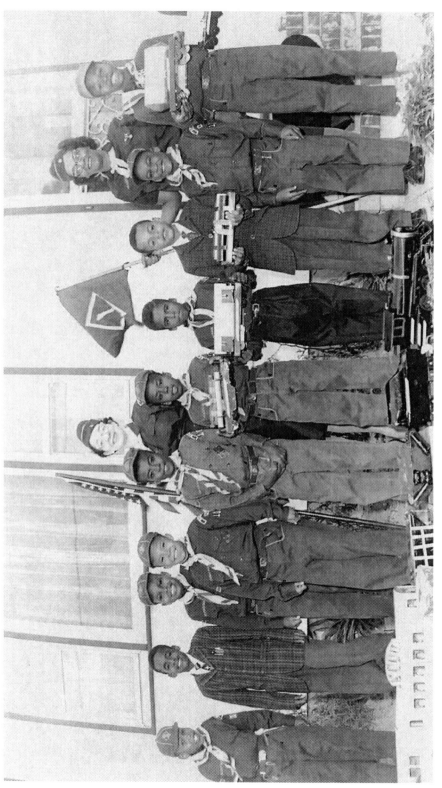

The churches in Asbury Park and Neptune were also used for hosting meetings for the local boys and girls scouts. Pictures are of some of Mrs. Hannon, an Asbury Park school teacher's troop members.

*They met then,
and they
still meet today.*

African Americans in Asbury Park organized. Community groups
consisted of social, fraternal, and church organization that contributed their time and resources to the betterment of our home town.
As far back as I can remember, groups called my father to take pictures at their annual planning meetings, or simply photograph their
members for one of the many historical programs and journals. The
Charms, the Links, Eastern Star, all of the Fraternity and Sorority
groups documented their planning and gifts to Asbury Park, and
Neptune, New Jersey.

Though I don't know what these groups were planning in these
photos, I do know that they were positive activities that produced
scholarships, funding for programs to benefit the needy, and spiri-
tual and educational leadership programs for their future leaders of
America.

*They met in living
rooms of member's
homes, they met at
the West Side
Community Center,
and at the various
lodges and lounges.*

Remember the names and deeds of the pioneers of Asbury Park: the Carter, Jone, Zachary, Deniels, Harris, Smith, Baker, Scott, Oates, Mitchell, Walker, Coleman, Morbley, Glover, Hood, Blue, and more: Write names in the borders of these pages and let the legacy of our Pioneer's and their commitments be documented.

Parade on Atkins Avenue, Asbury Park, 1950's -
Majorette is Janette Elmore-Johnson

*W*rite your memories here..

Parade on Springwood Avenue, Asbury Park, 1950's

Elks mortgage burning in the late 1950's.

*W*rite your memories here..

The little girl is Rosemary Swan. She is helping with the ritual of celebrating the burning of the organization mortgage. Asbury Park's Mayor Ray Kramer looks on as Mrs. Hughes looks on proudly. (*woman in middle of picture*). The woman on the left, is Mrs. Pleasant.

*W*rite your memories here..

Parade on Springwood Avenue, Asbury Park, 1950's - Majorette is Janette Elmore-Johnson

1950's Elks Parade on Springwood Avenue, Asbury Park, New Jersey

1950's Elks Parade on Springwood Avenue, Asbury Park, New Jersey

1950's Elks Parade on corner of Atkins and Springwood Avenue, Asbury Park.

1950's Elks Parade on corner of Atkins and Springwood Avenue, Asbury Park.

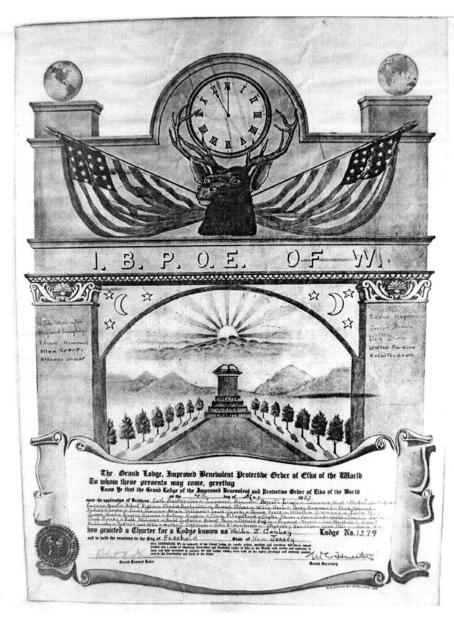

*W*rite your memories here..

1950's Elks Drill Team. Mr. Isaac Young is leader on the right front, also Principal of Bangs Avenue School in Asbury Park, NJ.

*W*rite your memories here..

Parade on Springwood Avenue, Asbury Park, 1950's

There is nothing like a parade!

The Asbury Park Elks marched pass my front door on Bangs Avenue one year. The people, the music, the fun and laughter!

The Pride of Asbury Park was every group of men, women, and children in their parade outfits.

*W*rite your memories here..

Colonel Raymond Harris from Atlantic City was the highlight at the Elk's Parade.
I remember his long and gentle giant strides as he marched in the summer heat.
The celebrations all ended at the Elks Lodge on Atkins Avenue.
Photo is of poor quality because of age damage.

I have hundreds of negatives of the people of Asbury Park enjoying their
Elks celebrations. This is just one of the early 1950 photographs. These
are the everyday people whose lives were cohesive because of their
belonging to this international organization that even today are contributors
to the African American society.

1957 Beauty Contest hosted by the New Jersey Association of the Masonic Lodge.

These two photographs from 1957 were taken at one of the many beauty contests that were hosted by the New Jersey State Association of the Masonic Lodge. The Masons were just one of the numerous social, fraternal, and African American organizations that I remember being proud of their African American beauties. In 1957, one of these ladies could have been Ms. America, or Ms. Universe, but the definition of beauty did not include them. They were intelligent, lovely, and above all, ladies of character.

The world's perception of black women has catapulted in forty-nine years from ugly remarks that we were black, and ugly, to being envied for our full features and our images are now desired and accepted. Putting on a bathing suit is just not traditionally something African American women did; and I believe, it wasn't because any one of these women liked to swim, or had the desire to be exhibitionist that these ladies braved it. It was because they wanted the world to know that they were just as beautiful as any other culture. This is just another area of having to prove ourselves acceptable and desirable. We are different, as is every one of God's creations. The reality, judging different cultures in beauty contest is like comparing apples to oranges, but they are all desirable. None are better, or more beautiful than the other.

1957 Beauty Contest contestant. unidentified woman

Another point that I get from looking at these old photographs, is that these ladies are all natural. When did we need to put yards of hair, miles of finger nails, and implanted this and that to be considered beautiful? I'll be glad when that phase in our life ends.

I don't know the names of these ladies, and I would love to add their names in my book: Asbury Park: A Westside Story. If you can identify these ladies, send their names to my address in the back of the book.

We can't all be the preacher's wife, but we can be strong, beautiful in our own images, faithful to the struggle and women's issues. Live life lovely, and leave good memories. The next time someone starts to take your picture, don't shy away, and say I don't like having my picture taken. Let the memory of the day be captured. Forty-nine years from now, someone will say, look at you…..how lovely.

1957 Beauty Contest hosted by the New Jersey Association of the Masonic Lodge.

Above: The Reindeer Rest on Springwood Avenue.

Right: A member of the Monmouth Lodge 122 of the Asbury Temple No.64 poses for a photo during one of their events.

Mt. Pisgah Church, Springwood Avenue, Asbury Park, NJ 60's

Pictured left to right are: Gary Bayliss, Vernis Williams, Calvin Plummer, James Powell, and yours truly Larry Lawson., Carol Williamson and Marcia Peek. On the front row: Rebecca Alexander, Dianna White, Willia Mae Williamson, Winifred Brown, Carol Grant, and Diane Manning.

Above: Seated first on left is Mrs. Letty Thoms. She was a well know artist from Long Branch, NJ. She is seated with organizers of the Cotillion Commitee for the 1953 Cotillion

1950's Cotillion at Convention Hall, Asbury Park, NJ

1950's Cotillion at Convention Hall, Asbury Park, NJ

1950's Cotillion at Convention Hall, Asbury Park, NJ

1950's Cotillion at Convention Hall, Asbury Park, NJ

1950's Cotillion at Convention Hall, Asbury Park, NJ

1950's Cotillion at Convention Hall, Asbury Park, NJ

1950's Cotillion at Convention Hall, Asbury Park, NJ

Monmouth County Cotillion 1950s
Convention Hall, Asbury Park, NJ

*W*rite your memories here..

Dr. Lorenzo Harris, Sr. makes prsentation Cotillion: 1960s
Convention Hall, Asbury Park, NJ

*W*rite your memories here..

This was a popular view on Springwood Avenue in the 1960's. Pictures from the wedding of the month would be placed in the rotating storyboard type display and people would gather to look at the new photos each week. I loved hearing the comments of the window lookers.

It was a great location for a photography studio. Eureka's Barber Shop, the Park's Drug and Liquor Store, B Evans Beauty Salon, Ruth Wise Beauty Salon, the Turf Club, and Elk Lodge across the street. People always wanted to capture the moment of their special events and the studio was convenient for them.

During the summer months, people were always walking from east to west or west to east on the Avenue. Residents of the Asbury Park Village, the Boston Way apartments, Lincoln Village, and other community dwellers came to Springwood Avenue to do their weekend food shopping, pick up their dry cleaning, have their shoes repaired, or pick up their medicine at the drug store. It was a lively community and the hundreds of faces that I saw as a young girl on "The Avenue" are forever in my mind.

Today, this area is being redeveloped. There are single family homes being built. It is a slow process, but eventually, everything that we remember about this lively area where African Americans lived, played and worked for a better life will be gone. Change is good. But we must never forget the contributions of the pioneer African American settlers. It was a place that was a blessing when there was nothing else; it was a start, when there were only beginnings; but most importantly, Springwood Avenue was the heart of the African American community that allowed people of many cultures to make gains on their individual designs of their promise land.

Lenora Carter oil painting portraits that Joseph Carter took during the 1960s.

Not only did my father take all of his pictures, he developed, retouched, and printed his work. In the 1960s, my Mother took a transparent oil painting class taught by the late artist, Letty Thoms, of Long Branch, NJ. She taught my mother how to paint black and white photographs that were first sepia toned, and mounted on a mat board. She would hand color them into beautiful life like oil painted portraits. She never gave up her first love of sewing, but in the evenings and on weekends, you would find her at her art table painting portraits. After my father passed away in 1980, she lost her heart for painting. Her last oil painted photograph was of Alicia Jones, of Neptune, NJ. I was learning how to take model portfolio photography, and she posed for me.

174

I have boxes of black and white 4x5 negatives of weddings, portraits, groups, and more from West Side of Asbury Park, NJ; some negatives, I still have not seen. Below: Photos in the waiting room of Carter's Photographic Studio when it was located at 1207 Springwood Avenue.

Golf in the 1960s in Asbury Park. This headliner golfer (Snead) came to Asbury Park to play in a benefit tournament at the Neptune City Country Club. My mother always loved golf, and played with my uncle George Niblack when she got a free moment.

Spring 1964 Asbury Park High School, on Sunset Avenue.

Winter 1964 Asbury Park High School, on Sunset Avenue.

*W*rite your memories here..

G. Edmond Smith, M.D., M.Ed., AAFP

A Family Physician, Community Educator, Researcher, and Author.

Publications:

Taking Care of Our Own: General Health Guide for African Americans (Release date—August, 2004—Hilton Publishing)

Weight Loss for African American Women: Eight Weeks to Better Health (Released November 1, 2001—Hilton Publishing)

Walking Proud: Black Men Living Beyond the Stereotypes (Released: April—2001) Dafina Books, a division of Kensington: New York, NY.

More Than Sex: Reinventing the Black Male Image (Released: January—2000)Kensington/Pinnacle Publishing: New York, NY.

Edmond had this photo taken at the Springwood Avenue Studio in the late 1960's.

One family I remember the most is the Smith Family. Edmond, Elaine, Brenda, Donna and Gary the twins, and Dennis. We played in the summer at the Bangs Avenue playground, ringing the bell swing for hours.. We played in the winter snow, and walked to school together each of my school days in Asbury Park.

Edmond is a success story out of Asbury Park. His writing is moving and healing, and a must read for every African American man and woman. I remember them as brilliant children, but when I read his book: Black Men Living Beyond the Stereotypes, I realized that I really didn't know their pain as children. As adults, we lost contact, but as children, they lived their live s so lovely, I only have good memories of them today that I cherish.

**Visit his web site: www. personaldoc.com
DrSmith@personaldoc.com (Email)**

"Grand Opening" Griffin Coin Operated Laundry on Springwood Avenue. 1960's.

*W*rite your memories here..

Photo looking East on Springwood Avenue. 1960s.

*W*rite your memories here..

Before the 1970 riots, a black man is photographed assisting a white man change a flat tire while watching police make an arrest on Springwood Avenue. (1960s)

*W*rite your memories here..

Springwood
Avenue
1960s

*W*rite your memories here..

Leo Karp's "Turf Club on the corner of Springwood and Atkins Avenue.

The Orchid Lounge: East end of Springwood Avenue was owned by Odyssey Moore.

*W*rite your memories here..

Hampton Inn, Big Bills, and the Zodiac was the Asbury Park and Neptune, NJ hot spot from the late 1950s through 1980s.

Andrew "Andy" L. Sanders and his brother William "Big Bill" Sanders. Andy graduated fromf Asbury Park High School. They both became businessmen owning and operating several small businesses at the Shore. They are also remembered for their Ice Cream Parlor, "Sunny Delight", a Convenience Store, and Barber Shop.

Wanting to keep a class act in operating a night club, they insisted a "No Pants worn by women rule". The community ladies were in an uproar, so the no pants rule was out. A few years later, they were one of the first to have Go-Go girls entertain their guests.

Ardently involved in sports, they were one of the first to install televisions in the bar area, and sponsored summer basketball games in a basketball court across the street from their bar.

Madonna's Bar - African Americans would gather there for fashion shows in the 50's. After the riots, they remained opened, but just as a bar and liquor store. They also sold lottery tickets.

1960s *F*ashion Show at the Elks Club in Asbury Park, NJ

This photo was taken on the corner of Springwood and Atkins Avenue. Looks like this family is waiting for the parade to start. In the background, you see Parks Drugs. Across the street, you see people standing on the second floor of the Turf Club. I don't remember it, but at one point in time, that building had two stories before a fire that reduced it to one floor.

*W*rite your memories here..

This photo was taken in the late 1940s. After a hard week's work, a night of dancing, and socializing was what people did to unwind. African American loved the night life. The "dark places" of the West Side, as described by people living across the track, were filled with people who were childhood friends. They had moved North at the same times to find better paying jobs and dwelling. The dancing, socializing, and drinking at the clubs was entertainment. They also served as a place where good news about job opportunities were exchanged. The bars and night clubs in Asbury Park acted as the Chamber of Commerce for people of color in the early days of the resort town, Asbury Park. Mixed networking was best done this way.

*W*rite your memories here..

The Youth of the 60's in Asbury Park, New Jersey

What has it been, forty-fifty years? We are still fighting for Equal Rights! The youth in this photo didn't have it. Today's youth, and youth from cities across American today, DO have it. They just have to show up to class, participate in positive activities, expose themselves to the world and all it has to offer, and do what ever it takes to be a part of today's competitive society.

The Asbury – Neptune Branch of the NAACP participated in a "March on Trenton" on October 26, 1963 which was before the summer of 1970 riots. Community leaders and other civic groups from the sister cities did the gathering with signs and chanted as they marched on their Capitol in Trenton, New Jersey. Their signs read: **Equal Rights Now**, **Equal Employment for ALL**, and proudly displayed their organization's names. Groups such as the *Asbury – Neptune Youth Council, NAACP*, MCAP, and various political action and ministerial alliances from neighboring cities participated.

In 1963, I attended Bond Street School. It was a new world for a seventh grader coming from Bangs Avenue School. I've always had a diversity of teachers, and classmates, but in the following year, the Asbury Park School System did a split session at the Asbury Park High School. Eighth graders attended school from 7 am to about 1:50 pm., and the second session starting in the afternoon until after 4:00 p.m. I don't remember the actual times, but what I do remember was hostility, exclusion, and subtle hate from adults and teenagers that made my high school days sometimes unbearable. My parents, family, friends, and my community icons gave me encouragement to get everything that I could get out of high school. I wasn't an A student, I was what they considered a "polite" C student. I was polite in order to control my temper, outrage of trying to overcome the preconceived attitudes of a young black girl and boys from the west side.

When I graduated from Asbury Park High School, I wrote in my year book, *"Remember All, Return to Recall All, Then Just Then…."* Just free writing on the inside cover of my class of '67 memory book; at the time, I didn't have a reason for writing that little phrase; but today, it is all clear. Maybe that is another book for me to write; but for now, writing "Asbury Park, A West Side Story has been a task opening a flood gate of memories that are bitter sweet and an awakening for me personally.

An Asbury Park/Neptune National Association for the Advancement of Colored People Life Member, Mrs. Hazel Greenwald receives a certificate from N.A.A.C.P. President Mrs. Katherine Harris, and unidentified NAACP member.

To say all of this, the political and social issues still unanswered or not meeting the standards of being FAIR or EQUAL that exist now were prevalent in the 1960's. Marching, or demonstrating as we called it was effective in perfecting these types of changes in the 1960's. It seemed even more effective when the masses of people originated from a multiple races and walks of life would participate together for mutual causes. But before us as African Americans, Blacks, or whatever we want to call ourselves, can join hands in making changes in society, we must re-knit the fabric that has become so loosely woven within our own culture. Our selective choices and tolerance levels for each other is as different as we are from one another. Organize and make clear our mutual acceptances of the changes that are needed to make our children valuable as more than simple consumers in America. There are so many issues we can address, but the main issue *for me* is still EDUCATION. If we must be in our community schools demographically more than 50% the population of any of the area schools, and we must be more than 50% considered economically disadvantaged, that does not mean that we should accept that the standards of education produce less than 33.3% in proficiencies in reading and even less in math. MARCH on the disparities as we did in the 60's to get EQUAL RIGHTS and EDUCATION from our city, county and state governmental officials.

The big question: WHO will march for the children who can't even get their parents to get out to the schools to support their children?

October 23, 1963
One month before the assassination of John F. Kennedy, the Asbury-Neptune NAACP Marched on in Trenton, New Jersey for Equal Rights and Education.

Change didn't come with out violence.

A note from a childhood friend from Asbury Park: *Frances Hartwell-Barnett*

Springwood Avenue -1960s

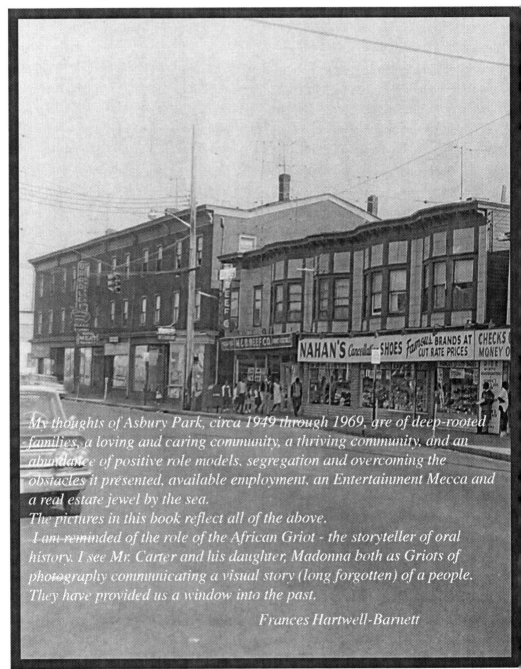

My thoughts of Asbury Park, circa 1949 through 1969, are of deep-rooted families, a loving and caring community, a thriving community, and an abundance of positive role models, segregation and overcoming the obstacles it presented, available employment, an Entertainment Mecca and a real estate jewel by the sea.

The pictures in this book reflect all of the above.

I am reminded of the role of the African Griot - the storyteller of oral history. I see Mr. Carter and his daughter, Madonna both as Griots of photography communicating a visual story (long forgotten) of a people. They have provided us a window into the past.

Frances Hartwell-Barnett

Asbury Park, New Jersey

On Springwood Avenue, 1960s: Frances Hartwell-Barnett and Albert Wade

The Viet Nam war touched thousands in the late 60s and 70s. This funeral is for one of the first to return home. I wasn't in New Jersey at the time, but I lost a classmate: Theodis Collins: Asbury Park High School Class of 1967.

St. Stephens African Methodist Episcopal Zion Church was located just off Springwood Avenue. It was demolished to build a new and modern church. I enjoyed feeling the warmth of a Sunday morning sun as it beamed through the colored glasses. I had my own personal bond with that church that I will forever hold dear to my heart. I always heard God on a whisper there.

With a war, civil, and social changes percolating, the 1970's were memorable and historical. The happiness and sadness that was shared by the world during the Viet Nam War, the Civil Rights issues, and my hair, which was the most drastic for me, it is a wonder the world survived.

I went from silky smooth, pageboy with bangs, to an afro that I wore for a period of time that took me on my own personal life's Merry Go Round.

I survived the 70's and 80's. That is another book in itself, but after my Father passed away in 1980, I was ready to do my own migrating, so I went South.

*W*rite your memories here..

197

This is Mt. Pisgah Lodge 48 FAMP.H.A. (Mason's Lodge)on Mattison Avenue that was located on the West Side. It was a popular place for local weddings and parties.

*W*rite your memories here..

Masonic Youth Club 1960's.

This is Danny Harris's Gas Station. 1950s

*W*rite your memories here..

Lots of two-three story homes were demolished to make room for development after the 1970 riots.

This house was located on the corner of Prospect and Bangs Avenue. It was demolished to erect the Bangs Avenue Middle School.

The 1970 Riots devastated the West Side. I remember the time, and have 8mm movies that my Mother took that night. My father asked that I never share them with anyone. In fact, he ask that I destroy them. The trashing of Springwood Avenue hurt him deeper than the fire that destroyed his studio in 1978.

These views were taken on the corner of Heck Street and Springwood Avenue and was taken in the late 1970's after the Riots.

Asbury Park -Neptune rival schools teamed up for community basketball teams. Donald Hammery, a community activist well know for his contribution to the youth of both towns. I remember some of the young men, because I graduated with some of them. Standing, left to right: Dwight Hammond, on the end is Donald Hammery. Kneeling left to right: Jessie Kendal. (1970) *Below*: David Parreott, Jr., Police Office, and Community Activist standing back row left poses with the first Asbury Park Middle School Football team.

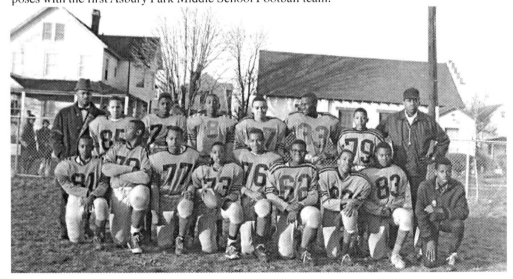

Pictured are some military men participating in a drawing for two brand new bikes.

MacDonalds Comes to the Shore

Cooking outside was always the treat in the summertime. Then fast food came to Asbury Park. MacDonalds! In the late 50's, my parents would take us for an evening ride in the car to cool off in the summer evening heat. We would first drive down Asbury Avenue toward the Beach. We would drive parallel the ocean and boardwalk. It seemed like miles while we drove all the way to Lake Avenue which turned into Springwood Avenue. I can still see all of the people, and lights of the city. Heading west on Springwood to Highway 35, we would pull into MacDonald's and you would think we never had a French-fry before. We would share two small bags between the five of us. For some reason, those two small bags of fries were just enough. Today, I eat a supersized box by myself. Well, I use to.

Madonna's Bar and Liquor Store was located on the last block east on Springwood Avenue. In the early 1950, Madonna's was one of the favoirte nightclub spots for music, fashion shows and social gathering.

*W*rite your memories here..

Robert's Shoe Service.

*W*rite your memories here..

*Hats
are always in.*

Fashions in the 1950's.

Elks fashion show, late 1960's.

I loved the beautiful stained glass windows of St. Stephens African Methodist Episcopal Zion Church. The mahogany altar always glistened. Most of my friends went there so I visited often. This church was demolished, and was replaced by a beautiful building on Springwood Avenue. It was one of the oldest churches in the community dating back to the late 1800's.

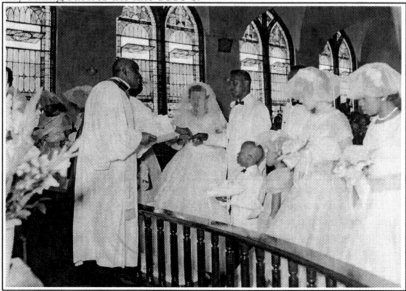

Pictured left to right: *Easter Sunday after everyone had their pictures taken at the studio. Ernest, Madonna, and Joseph Carter. 1050's*

*M*y treasures of nostalgic photography by my father, Joseph Carter, takes us to the celebration of Easter in Asbury Park in the late 1940s and 50s. The weather was so unpredictable. You didn't know what you were going to get until Easter morning. It could be snow flurries, or a china blue sky, but a cold day. It would be just cold enough, forcing out a winter coat to ruin the spring colored outfit that was purchased especially for Easter Sunday. Then, there were those perfect Sunday mornings that brought in the pre-summer excitement of wearing bright colors, and going to the Boardwalk.

The barber shops on Springwood Avenue were filled with boys and men of all ages getting that fresh hair cuts. Every mother and daughter made appointments with their favorite beauticians; if not, mothers were washing, pressing, and curling their daughter's hair the night before Easter. Keeping Shirley Temple curls and processed hairdos intact while sleeping was a task. It was a wonder anyone got any sleep the Eve of Easter.

The weekend before Palm Sunday to that Saturday before Easter, the hustle and bustle on Cookman Avenue would remind you of Christmas Eve. The shopping lists included a pair of spanking brand new shinny black or white paten leather shoes, taffeta dresses, with matching pocket books, gloves, and an Easter hat covered with silk flowers. For the boys, a new pair of shoes, a suit for the big boys, and short pants for little boys. Clip-on bow ties and white ankle length sock with lace were always in high demand. Parents made sure the little ones had on clean socks to go shopping in Asbury Park at *Lerner Shops*, *J. J. Newberry*, the *Asbury Youth Center* and *Steinbach's Department Store*. On Springwood Avenue, there was Fisch's Clothing store, and Nahan's Shoe Store. These are just a few that are remembered.

Shopping for Easter Clothes Downtown Asbury Park: An unexpected snow store didn't put a damper on the Easter Shopping.

When Easter Morning came, first on the agenda were sunrise services at the beach and community churches. *St. Peter Claver Catholic Church* on the corner of Springwood and Ridge Avenue was always well attended Palm and Easter Sunday. Ahh... *to Reminisce Easter Sunday in Asbury Park.*

I can't believe I haven't found any photographs taken on the boardwalk at the Easter Parade or the Easter Egg hunt that the City sponsored each year. I don't even have memories of going to the Parade. I'll continue my search through my Dad's collection.

I have hundreds of Easter Sunday family portraits. Maybe that is why I don't remember ever going to an Easter Parade. We had the parade right there in the middle of our living room when Carter's Photo Studio was located at 1521 Bangs Avenue in the 50s. Prior to that, the studio was located on Springwood Avenue next door to the State Pool Room. In the 60s the studio was located at 1207 Springwood Avenue and I do remember being the little receptionist and photographer's assistant for dozen's of Easter Sunday portraits of children, and their families.

At the end of the day, my family would go to the boardwalk and eat cotton candy, and candy apples and the best popcorn in the world. We would ride the Merry-Go-Round and try hard to get that golden ring. I loved the Ferris Wheel the best. I loved having the bird's eye view to watch all the beautiful people of all races enjoying the holiday and seeing people feeling reborn and free after a cold winter.

In 1978, a fire destroyed our studio that was located at 715 Madison Avenue. Hundreds of negatives were lost in that terrible fire along with the memories of historic events such as the First African American to actually win the Easter Parade, and the first African American Judges that participated from the West Side. In 1976, Carl Williams of Mr. Fashion's Men's Cloths, and a Neptune, NJ resident, Puff Smith were selected as judges. Photos or not, we have the memories. It has always been wonderful to reminisce Easter on the West Side.

A Family Portrait in the City -1940's
It wasn't uncommon for someone to stop my dad on the streets to have their picture taken. Here is the VanHuff family posing for a family portrait on Easter Sunday. Carter's Studio customers were loyal.

1978 Fire

The 715 Mattison Avenue, Morris Buildong was destroyed by a fire that started in the basement of the four story office building.

Carter's Photographic Studio, Klitzman, Klitzman, and Gallaher Law Office, Abrams Dentistry, and other business lost everything within a few hours as the fire raged like an inferno. (Asbury Park Press Photo)

Joseph Carter is comforted by his wife, Lenora (left) and daughter, Donna, as his photography studio is lost in fire in Morris Building, Asbury Park.

Studio Burned Out

I remember the clipping form the Asbury Park Press in 1978. My father's life's work was going up in flames and he had a smile on his face. The material things that were lost were not what he missed; it was the memories he documented for the community that he cherished and missed the most. Later, we spent hours just looking at the old negatives that were saved.

The Morris Building located at 715 Mattison Avenue was totally destroyed on this day, but my Father had the same enthusiasm about opening a new studio that he had the day he opened his first studio on Springwood Avenue in 1947. With the camera he had on his shoulder, a few pieces of equipment that he had at home, and a gift from photographer friends that he had made over the years, he was able to open a studio within a month a block east at 513 Mattison Avenue.

Darkroom that was distroyed in the 1978 Fire

Photography was more than just a living for my dad, it was also his hobby. His collection of old cameras and darkroom equipment was also completly destroyed.

A beautiful oil painting of Lenora Carter that was painted by Letty Thoms, an Artist from Long Branch, NJ . This oil painting was my favorite piece of art that was lost in the fire of 1978.

715 Mattison Avenue, Asbury Park, NJ- The Morris Building 1970

Sylvia Klitzman-Bressler, the eldest sister of the Klitzman's Family and her husband, Sam Bressler. She told me stories of the Nazi concentration camps and her family's heritage. On Jewish holidays, she shared their meaning. I've always appreciated her instructions. She respected my father's ambition and dedication to his family.

In the late 1960's to 1980, Joseph Carter did documentation photography for the law firm of Klitzman, Klitzman, and Gallagher. Their assignments required him to photograph the streets of Asbury Park, Neptune, and neighboring communities that documented the scenes of automobile accidents, and various negligent type legal cases. Most of the photography that was taken during that period was destroyed by the 1978 fire.

The studio was relocated from 1207 Springwood Avenue location just after the 1970 riots. Prior to moving into the Morris Building, I packed my fathers oldest negatives and stored them in the basement of our home on Bangs Avenue. It is ironic, that the studio was not destroyed during the riots that devastated so many businesses on the Avenue.

I worked as a receptionist for the Law firm in the late 70s, and did photography off and on for them after my dad passed away in 1980. Sylvia Bressler called herself my Jewish mother. She shared a wealth of knowledge about appreciating the heritage and roots of all cultures in addition to the arts of secretarial science. Her brothers, Abraham, and Charles Klitzman gave my father an opportunity to show his talents and skills. He soon had accounts with several local legal firms, and area businesses after references made by the Klitzmans.

214

The Klitzman's of Asbury Park: L to R husband of Anne Klitzman-Levy, her brother, Charles and Abraham Klitzman.

Trees for Israel

כי תבואו אל הארץ ונטעתם (ויקרא יט,כג)
AND WHEN YE SHALL COME INTO THE LAND AND YE SHALL PLANT *(Leviticus 19, 23)*

Trees Have Been Planted
In Memory of Your Beloved Husband
Joseph W. Carter

By Ray Kramer
Mayor, Asbury Park
Director Freeholder
Monmouth County

Jewish National Fund   קרן קימת לישראל   two trees

...and when ye shall come into the land and ye shall plant (Leviticus 19:23)

Joseph A. Carter, Sr. passed away April 3, 1980 at Monmouth Medical Center in Long Branch, NJ after a short illness. He died of pancreas cancer six weeks after diagnosis. The Mayor of Asbury Park and Director Freeholder of Monmouth County, Ray Kramer, planted two trees in memory of my father. The certificate from the Trees of Israel was issued by the the Jewish National Fund (Karen Kayemeth LeIsrael), 42 East 69th Street, New York, NY. 10021. RE 1277-50

The Carter's 1958

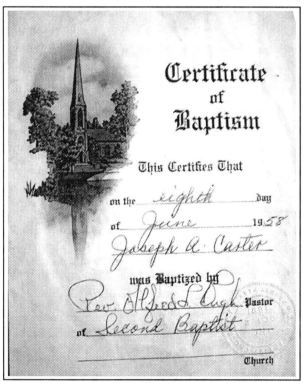

*M*y father never attended any one church in Asbury Park, but he made his children go to church. I remember him being Baptized in 1958. He and my Mother never went to church again, but insisted that their children go. He didn't say where, we just had to go to a " Church" on Sunday morning.

I attended several churches. God protected me as a child, and is still guiding my steps today - *All because my parents made us keep an open mind about faith.*

I've learned that the common denominator of all churches is loving one another.

Certificate of Baptism of *Joseph A. Carter, Sr.* - 1958 - Second Baptist Church, Asbury Park, NJ Reverend Pugh

*1960
Youth Advocate
Awards
Presented to
Asbury Park
Business, and
Civic Leaders.*

*Just before going to press, I received this letter from a pioneer Asbury Park businessman,
writer, and photographer.*

JOSEPH CARTER WAS AN EXTRAORDINARY PHOTOGRAPHER
By Frank C. Vecchione

I read the article "Happy Father's Day: Asbury
Park: contributed by Joseph Carter's daughter,
Madonna Carter Jackson in your June 2006 Issue of
the Shore African American magazine with interest.
It brought back my many memories of Joe when he
was my photo finisher when I dealt with
photography back in the 1960's and until Joe's
death in 1980. I would rank Joe among the best
photographers in New Jersey. His knowledge of
photography was endless.

I enjoyed his friendship and he gave me quite a
few tips in photography. My knowledge in that
field would fill Joe's pinky on one of his hands. I
have read about Joe Carter in the past describing
him as a West Side photographer of Asbury Park. It
bothered me to describe him that way. He was not
only a photographer of all of Asbury Park, but it
should include Monmouth County and all of New
Jersey.

Joe's last office and Lab was on Mattison
Avenue, across the street from the former Asbury
Park Press building in Asbury Park. He lived on the
corner of Ridge and Bangs Avenues in Asbury and
he had a second Lab in the cellar of his house. At the
other end of the cellar was a small brightly-lit
bandstand with colorful rugs on the wall and a drum
set in the middle. Earnest" Boom" Carter, his son,

built it. Joe was a great supporter of his son and
knew he was a talented drummer. Earnest went on
to play drums for Bruce Springsteen and David
Sancious. Bruce Springsteen, before he made the big
time, rehearsed in the cellar a few times. Joe
introduced me to Bruce Springsteen one night when
I went to pick up some of my work. This was
before he made it in the big time. I was in Joe's
Mattison Avenue office one day and Joe pointed to
a TIME magazine on his coffee table in his lounge
and there was Bruce Springsteen on the cover. He
reminded me that he introduced Bruce to me in his
cellar sometime ago. Joe

Joe had been involved in many important events.
He was the Official Photographer of the New
Jersey Boat Show that operated out of the
Convention Hall in Asbury Park. He did work for
many lawyers. His work included a photo shot
from a plane that was instrumental for a Law Firm
to win a million-dollar case. He did work for Police
Departments, Walter Reade theaters and many other
businesses.

Joe was well liked by many people of all walks
of life and was respected by many photographers.

-Shore African American Magazine October 2006
Letter to the editor:

42

Years of
Marriage
Mr. & Mrs.
Hunt of Hunt's
Funeral Home
celebrate my
parents 42nd
Anniversary.

Mr. James Hunt was a well respected businessman and civic leader in the Shore Area. There are many photographs of families' loved ones that were taken just before their funerals. Friends and family members that could not come to the funeral were always very appreciative to have these tastefully produced photographs.

Conrad Lyons published the "Spotlite," a monthly pictorial magazine covering the East Side of Asbury Park. She covered the political and socialite events and Joseph Carter processed her film and printed her stock photos. What a collection she must have had of the people of Asbury Park during her years.

Conrad Lyons of Spot Lite Magazine, Tom Gasque, NJ Boat Show
and Convention Hall event planner at Anniversary Party.

Joe Carter was the New Jersey Boat Show's official photographer for several years. He was instrumental in the selection of the first African American **"Miss Boat Show Queen"** at Asbury Park's Convention Hall. I was not able to find those photos of **Ms. Dorothy White**, but I will, and will highlight her in one of my future magazine articles.

1950 Weddings

House Weddings and Receptions were very popular in the 1950's. There were places like the St. Peter Claver Hall, the Masonic Temple, Elks Club, and the Reindeer Rest that African Americans held their receptions and banquets.

*W*rite your memories here..

220

On the corner of Springwood and Ridge Avenues, the St. Peter Claver Catholic Church was the popular place to see some of the most beautiful weddings. Brides and Grooms sporting convertibles, tuxes, and gowns made for a prince and princess.

Across the street from the church was a two story building that had a huge hall for banquets and receptions. On Friday nights, there were Canteens for the young people in the community. The lower level was sometimes used for Bar-B-Q's by the Robert's Family , and yard type sales.

Being situated only yards from the City of Neptune, making it the Avenue's entrance to the West Side Asbury Park.

221

Social clubs sponsored fund raisers for their organization. There was always a "Dance" scheduled at one of the Halls, Community Center, Berkley, Carver, or one of the Lodges.

Area business like the Walburn Sewing Factory that was located on the corner of Monroe and Rail Road Avenue employed all nationalities who wanted to work. At the end of the year, groups posed for the annual group photo.

When my father passed away in 1980, my shelter disappeared. My world was no long being seen through censored, rose colored glasses. I wanted to do some of the things that he wanted me to do. This is typical of most young people starting out on their own, not wanting their parents to design their paths, but during the last six weeks of my fathers life, he coached me in continuing the studio. He quizzed me in darkroom, lighting, chemistry, and selecting various types of photographic paper. It was a six week crash course in running a professional photographic studio. He told me that it would not cost much. "Just get a small place, work part time at first, and then fly," he said. I did for a while, but I had my personal directions that I wanted to explore. I stayed in New Jersey long enough to make sure my Mother was situated, then I did my own migration, but South.

While still in Asbury Park, I opened a studio at 715 Mattison Avenue, soon after, I moved to 1303 Memorial Drive. This is when I tried to publish a black oriented pictorial magazine. With Constance Irby-Holmes as my co-publisher, we gave birth to EXPOSURE MAGAZINE 1981

Pre-schoolers from the ICCC staff for Black History Week

First Exposure Magazine 1980

Front cover: April 1981
Exposure Magazine

I always knew that the shore area had African Americans that were doing more than the negative news that the Asbury Park Press was releasing every day. I know the bad news has to be told, but there was never any good news. Never any motivating and positive images for our children of color to see. Our first cover featured Neptune High School's Scarlet Fliers IV Champions.

On the cover of the eighth cover was Mr. Lucious Zachary of Asbury Park. Most people knew him as the fashion coordinator for Dainty Apparel clothing store, but

**NEPTUNE FLIERS
CHEERLEADERS**

also a Carnegie Hall performer in 1956 where he performed at Carnegie Hall. He has performed in LaTosca at the Paramount theater, and with the Metro Lyric Opera of the Monmouth Opera Guild. At the time we used him for our cover, he was a teacher at the Bangs Avenue Middle School, and singing with the Temple Beth El in Oakhurst under the direction and service of Rabbi Shulmen.

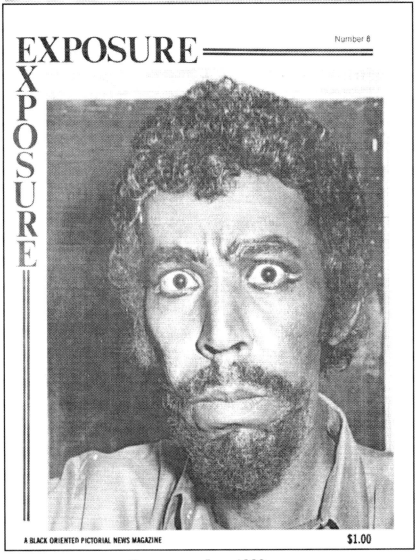

Front cover: June 1982
Exposure Magazine

*W*rite your memories here..

_____

_____

_____

_____

The Ahmar Hizean Junior Karate Team, instructed by **Mr. James Long**, demonstrated their talents at the West Side Community Center on Thanksgiving Day. **Mr. Charles Vernon**, a commercial artist, displayed color portraits and hand painted sweatshirts.

TELL EVERYONE ABOUT *EXPOSURE*

Wedding Bells

Forston-Harris

Ann Harris, Neptune, and **O.D. Fortson**, Neptune, were married in Neptune on December 5, 1981 with **Rev. R.C. Goodman** officiating.

Honor attendants were **Mrs. Iva Adams**, Matron of Honor, **Mr. Nicholas Fortson**, the grooms brother, was best man.

An intimate family dinner was hosted at the Ft. Monmouth NCO Club.

The couple will reside in Neptune.

ANNOUNCEMENTS

Cladston and Icilma Eswick of Neptune, celebrated their 50th Wedding Anniversary. A dinner in their honor was given in Hillside, N.J. and attended by their children, family and friends.

SEASON GREETINGS AND A PROSPEROUS NEW YEAR

*W*rite your memories here..

Front cover: December1981
Exposure Magazine

*W*rite your memories here...

OUTPUT

a message from the publishers

It has been over a year since the first issue of EXPOSURE Magazine was published and as we go into our second year we urge you again to get involved with us in this much needed source of communication.

We, as publishers, have tried to create a strong community link through the exposure of the positive achievements of individuals, businesses, churches and organizations in the Monmouth/Ocean County area.

It has been our feeling that the news media considers Black news good news only when it is negative and therefore covers very few positive achievements of individuals and groups in the community.

EXPOSURE Magazine offers you a source of communication that is much needed in the Black community—keeping you informed of who is doing what, when and where. THIS IS YOUR COMMUNITY INFORMATION GUIDE.

EXPOSURE MAGAZINE is published bi-monthly and will cover your 1982 calendar of events throughout Monmouth County.

Again we urge you to get involved in your community by keeping us informed of all activities, special programs, social affairs and by submitting pertinent information that you think will be of service to the community.

We are looking forward to a very eventful year with EXPOSURE MAGAZINE at your service.

Madonna C Lindsey
Madonna Carter Lindsey

Constance Irby
Constance Irby

Opinions expressed by the writers are their own and do not necessarily reflect the view of the management of this magazine, nor does the management accept the responsibility for any writer's opinion.

This publication comes to you with the support of our many wonderful advertisers. When you patronize them, be sure to tell them:

EXPOSURE

sent you.
They'll be glad you did.
(And so will we.)

**Madonna Carter Lindsey
Constance Irby**
PUBLISHERS & EDITORS

Madonna Carter Lindsey
PHOTOGRAPHER

Constance Irby
TYPOGRAPHER

*Printed by West Branch Graphics
Long Branch, N.J.*

Distributed by:
EXPOSURE
P.O. Box 167
1303 Memorial Drive
Asbury Park, N.J. 07712

Telephone:
DAYS
(201) 774-2775 or 988-8730

EVENINGS
(201) 542-8913 or 988-6809

Printed in U.S.A. Subscription rates: $5.50 for 6 issues.

EXPOSURE MAGAZINE is published by Exposure Enterprises, P.O. Box 167, 616 Madison Avenue, Asbury Park, N.J. 07712, (201) 774-2775/988-8730, for informative purposes. It is designed exclusively for the Black community serving as a community information guide of what is going on and who is doing it. Copyright 1981 by Exposure Enterprises. No part of this publication may be duplicated without the express written permission of Exposure Enterprises.

4   EXPOSURE/JUNE, 1982

Editorial Page of First Anniversary Issue: June 1982
Exposure Magazine

*W*rite your memories here..

....

....

....

....

Front cover: October 1981
Exposure Magazine

Exposure Magazine interviewed people like:
Singer and Actress, Eartha Kitt and Gil Noble, TV News Anchor-man., but our goal was to make celebrities out of our own community people.

Front cover: August 1981
Exposure Magazine

Exposure Magazine interview:

Smith Institute of Cometology of Asbury Park, New Jersey. Exposure Magazine held its first graduation in August 1981. Mrs. Beverly Smith, founder and president. The first graduates awarded diplomas were: Ms. Clarice Rodriquez, Valedictorian, Ms. Michelle Boykins, Ms. Darlene Clark, Ms. Dorothy Conway, Mr. William Gutheridge, Ms. Leola Henry, Ms. Julia Jones, Ms. Lily Mitchell, Ms. Abby Pearman, Ms. Elmira Smith, Ms. Connie Vann, and Ms. Delores Wilson.

The Monmouth County and the City of Asbury Park have the honor of being the home of the second Black Beauty Culture School to open its doors in the State of New Jersey.
Back cover: August 1981
Exposure Magazine

★ ★ ★ NIGHT CLUB SCENE ★ ★ ★

Miss Eartha Kitt
Comes To Asbury Park

The Club Atlantis featured **Miss Eartha Kitt** for the 4th of July holidays. Miss Kitt, fluent in eight languages, wowed the crowd with her smash hits "I Want To Be Evil," "Guess Who I Saw Today" and "Champagne Taste."

Performing to a packed house, Miss Kitt received a standing ovation for her rendition of "All By Myself" — a song for which she wrote a personal and stirring poem to her daughter a few years ago.

As shown in the sequence of pictures, Miss Kitt lends many moods to her songs. A person of extraordinary warmth, she posed with EXPOSURE photographer **Madonna Lindsay**, Atlantis owners **George Chamlin, Maxine Sabin and Fran Remus** and with **Councilman Lorenzo Harris** who welcomed Miss Kitt to the city.

Exposure Magazine interview

Dr. Lorenzo Harris welcomed Ms. Kitt to the City of Asbury Park in August 1981. She is a person of extraordinary warmth. She performed at the Atlantis, owners George Chamlin, Maxine Sabin and Fran Remus. So now....we have celebrities in this book. Ms. Kitt was down to earth and real off stage.

233

Exposure Magazine interview
A graduate of Asbury Park High School Class of 1944. A pioneer to Asbury Park and Neptune, Mr. Floyd R. Scott, Jr., who is the Architectural Designer of the Asbury Park Municipal Building . He is Monmouth County's first Black fighter pilot with the 332nd Fighter Group during World Ward II. First African American to ever be elected to public office in the 77 year history of Neptune Township Board of Education.

Dr. Scuddie, and Sarah McGee

The shore area has positive images and mentors to remember: Dr. Scuddie, and Sarah McGee, Howard West, Rev. Thomas & Mrs. Pearl Thomas, Floyd Scotts, Taylors, Rev. Rufus Goodman, The Daniel Family, Thomas Smith Sr. & Jr., The Hoods, The Zachary's, The Dr. Lorenzo Harris, the Hunt Family, Galloway, Bakers, Hamm, Sheltons, Parreotts, Brantley's Coles,Mr. & Mrs. Lawrence Robinson, Vernon McGowen, Irby-Holmes, Baitey's, The Scale's Family, Jesse Galloway, Sharon Harris,Gunter's, Wilson's, Dorothy Dallah, Zeresh Bass, Willie Mae Blue, Joyce Phillips, Irma Meade, Vernice McGee, Robert and Ann Cooper, Holland's, Duck's, Carter's, Jones', Coleman's, the Thom's Family, Seawright's, Carl Williams, Samuels, Willie Hamm, Carol Kelly, O'Neill's, Blackwel's, the Bullocks, Sanders,Dorothy Mc McNIsh, Puff Smith, Dr. Michael Brantley, Hilda Cambell, Anne Baker, Dave and Olla Parreott, Rosalind Seawright, Larrick Daniels, Bob Farley, Gary Smith, Whittaker's,Synovia Britt-Simms, Niblacks, Bookers, Richardson's, Judy Holland Bess, Crystal Brown, Cheryl Parker, Pearl Coleman, Virginia Newkirk, Jefferson's, Jackson's, and every member of the **NAACP.**

At an NAACP Luncheon are honored guests L to R: Joe Taylor, community activist, Anne Baker, teacher and Director of the Intercommunity Child Care Association posed with ABC's co-anchor Gil Noble, host of the black public affairs series "Like It Is".

History continues.......

July 2006 - One year has passed since the first issue of the Shore African American Magazine was published. After seeing the first issue, I knew that I wanted to be a part of their project. The Publisher Robert Harrison, and Co-Publisher, Constance "Connie" Holmes welcomed my input to their publication, and I have provided an insert every issue since.

Constance Irby-Holmes and Robert Harrison, Publishers

Constance Holmes   *Robert Harrison*

Opposite page: Asbury Park/Neptune N.A.A.C.P. members: Vernon McGowen, Howard West, President, Reverend Jack Thomas, Michael Babatunde Olatunji, NAACP Award's African American Service Award recipient , James Scales, Mrs. Pearl Thomas, Maxine Daniels, Henrietta Zachary, Tom Danials, and Floyd Scott. (1980)

Shore African American Magazine

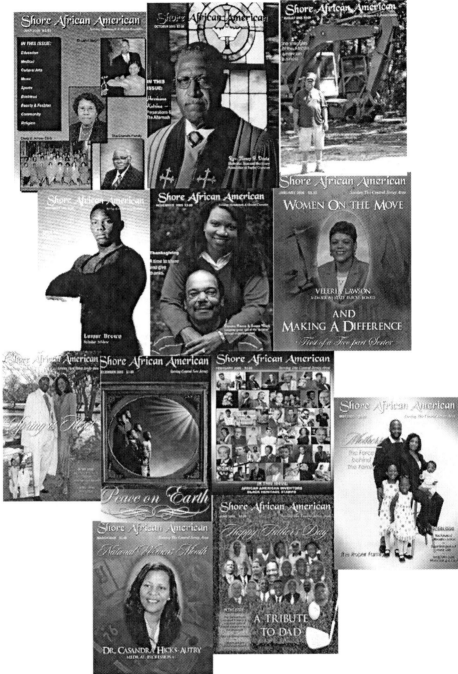

Contact:
Shore African American Magazine
601 Bangs Avenue, Suite 400
Asbury Park, NJ 07712

Serving the Central Jersey Area
Asbury Park, New Jersey

Acknowledgments

I want to say a special thank you to Connie Holmes, Co-publisher for the Shore African American Magazine (SAA), for allowing me to be a part of their publication that will be celebrating their first year's anniversary on July 2006. To Robert Harrison, Publisher of SAA, I say thank you and that I hope that your venture with publishing and capturing the memories of our community is successful and that it be a long lived adventure. There is a childhood friend and classmate, Frances Hartwell Bennett who stimulated my memories about our home town. We shared many emails and telephone calls while cross referencing information about people and organizations in the pictures. It is amazing how many people and their family members she remembers. Mrs. Denise Hawkins, General Chairperson of the Monmouth County Cotillion Committee, Inc., who was so gracious in responding to my request for historical information about past Cotillions. The organization's program journals provided names of people and businesses that helped with my research about old Asbury Park. Reverend David Parreott, former Asbury Park police officer for he and his wife Olla's wonderful memories and reflections on our hometown. To Helen Pike, author of several publications about Asbury Park for her encouragement to tell my west side story. Rainette B. Holimon is passionate about preserving the history and images of Asbury Park's West Side through maps and presentation, I thank you for your generosity in editing my second printing. The greatest of my appreciation goes to all of the people, businesses, and organization, who used Carter's Photographic Studio over the years. My father was a self trained photographer who did everything he could to provide the best quality service within his means to capture the memories of the community he cared so much for. Lastly, Outskirts Press, Inc. Without them, there would be no Asbury Park: A West Side Story.

Time passes, photographs and negatives disintegrate, so it has been my mission to preserve these historical and treasured memories from Asbury Park. During the process of collecting information about the people and places in this book, I realize that this story is not just about the City of Asbury Park, but about human beings who would otherwise be forgotten, leaving another missing link in all of our history. No matter whether this book holds any ones interest other than my own. Maybe in another 25 or 50 years from now, someone will look at this book and remember someone in their family who told them stories about Asbury Park, New Jersey.

I expect and hope that I will get lots of letters and calls from readers recollecting memories of their friends or family members in this collection of photographs, or of reminisces of organizations featured in this book. Possibly within a few years I will reprint, adding unidentified person's names, and the communications I receive. If not, it would certainly be good material for my monthly article in the Shore African American Magazine.

Until then, as my father would say, *"Live Life Lovely, and Leave Good Memories."*

I have boxes and boxes of 4x5 Black and White negatives that I have not viewed. I guess there will be another book one day; but for now, this has been my stroll down memory lane through the eyes of my father's photography. Each photo has a story that I will always remember.

My Mother, Lenora Niblack Carter suggested that I find another method of processing these negatives without the use of photographic chemicals. I would have probably destroyed all of the negatives had it not been for the new digital technology. I photographed each negative and used a desktop publishing software to create a digital photograph. The images you see are direct from the negative, some without the retouching and special efects my Father provided through darkroom techniques. It would have been just too costly for me to have each photo processed using the traditional darkroom methods, and I hope that you enjoy the images regardlesss of their condition or quality. Over the past twenty-four years, I have moved south carrying my boxes of Asbury Park treasures, and Garland, my husband, made sure I didn't lose one negative to the cruel elements of storage. I thank and appreciate him for all his help making this publication a reality for me.

If you recognize any of the unidentified people, or know a little history about a photograph in Asbury Park: A West Side Story, *I would love to hear from you.*

Tell me the page number, and give a brief discription of the picture. Either write, or email me at the following addresses:

Madonna Carter Jackson
P O Box 30292
Columbia, SC 29203

or email me at:
madonnaj@bellsouth.net

Joseph A. Carter, Sr., and his daughter, Madonna 1950

In 1949, our family moved to 1521 Bangs Avenue. Dr. Sebastian Vaccaro was born in that house and his Mother passed away there. During the winter of 1949, I was hospitalized with pneumonia, and Dr. Vaccaro said that the damp environment at the 1137 Springwood Studio apartment would be fatal for both me and my brother. He gave my father his brother's telephone number and told him to tell his brother that he recommended that he rent their old house to our family. My mother was delighted. She wanted a real home for her family. She made drapes for every window in that two story house. The living room had four windows, the dining room had four in addition to the background drapes that were used for the studio. Those long ivory white drapes covered the full wall of the dining room area. My parents made our house a studio during business hours, and a loving home when the studio was closed.

The house was on the northeast corner or Ridge and Bangs Avenues, and is one block west of Bangs Avenue School. It was less than fifty feet from the Neptune/Asbury Park city line. I grew up with friends from both towns. There were American Indians, Italians, Cubans, Spanish and Hispanics, African Americans, Greeks and more within our one square mile city limits.

By the time my brother and I were ready to enter school in 1951-52, the world was healing from depression and wars. African Americans were attending college, and graduating with Medical, Business Administrative, and Education Degrees. Even though discrimination was still ravaging the south, it was at another level in the north. My parents were so busy making a living, making sure that food was on the table every night, and clothes and shoes were suitable, that higher education was not a thought for them, but it was a dream they had for their children.

My father's career as a photographer rendered a respectable salary, and my mother worked as seamstress in a coat factory for over twenty years. They were resourceful, and made sure that there was never a day we felt hungry or poor. We never felt less because of their lack of education. We grew up in a society that made my father feel that we had to embrace the diversity of our world, and understand the cultures and religions outside of our own. "Expose yourself to a little of everything before you condemn or judge; but most of all, be a respectful, decent human being."

Growing up in Asbury Park, I was able to observe behavioral correctness and incorrectness, and the moral values as defined by the over thirty-two churches that were within our one square mile city of Asbury Park. My exposure to life in Asbury Park by living and seeing the deeds of the pioneers of a town whose people were striving to survive in a changing world has made me grateful for my life experiences.

I don't judge the world, but I have learned you must live life lovely as my father did, and try to leave good memories. Take pictures of your life, no matter what you look like. Twenty-five years from now, you will have your own book of your life to share with the future generations.

Asbury Park: A West Side Story

KENNETH A. GIBSON
MAYOR
NEWARK, NEW JERSEY
07102

April 8, 1980

Mrs. Lenora Carter
1521 Bangs Avenue
Asbury Park, New Jersey

Dear Mrs. Carter:

When we have lost someone who is dear to us, the only
solace to be found is to try to understand that this,
also, is a part of life.

I hope that you, your family and friends will find
that understanding which will sustain you through
your grief.

You have my deepest sympathy.

Sincerely,

Kenneth A. Gibson

KAG:cg

*Death is simply living
through memory.
Live life lovely, and
leave good memories.*

*Thank you for the
memories Daddy.*

*Joseph A. Carter, Sr.
Photographer
1917-1980*